Building Brain Power

Written &
Illustrated by

Ann McGee-Cooper

DEDICATION

To my mother, Georgia Clara Bowen Ulrich, who sets a daily example for creativity, courage, risking, caring and pace setting.

One evening at dinner, Mother announced that in a few months she would be forty. She had never learned to ride a bicycle and thought she would set a goal to learn before her fortieth birthday. My brother tried valiently to talk her out of this new adventure on the grounds that it might be too danger-ous for "a woman of her age." I quickly chimed in but we were both wasting our breath. She was not to be deterred. She would learn to ride a bicycle!

My brother and I were both teenagers looking out for our own interests and not at all sincerely con-cerned about our mother's safety. We were both afraid of being teased by our friends and I was imagining the dents and scratches my new bicycle would suffer.

One evening, again at dinner, sporting a scraped knee and bruised elbow she announced, "I learned some-thing today. Whatever I look at I run into! I have to be careful not to look at any of the neighbors while I ride."

In spite of all our lack of support, Mother was proudly riding my blue bicycle weeks before her deadline. I had little appreciation for the precious gift she was giving to us at that time. In fact I did all I could to change her to a course less courageous (and, of course, less embarrassing for me). But she perservered. And now, thirty years later, I want to thank her for the role model she continues to provide.

ACKNOWLEDGMENTS

This book culminates twenty-nine years of teaching and reflects the learning process of the teacher along the way. All those who were my mentors, my students, many parents of students...contributed to my growth and to them I am indebted.

I give special thanks to the Hunting Family; Shirley, David, Martha, Randy, Carol and Al, and to my son, Rayo McCollough, who helped develop the original set of Brain Builders.

Another special group of people helped in putting the book together with special care. Betty Wehrle, Jackie Maxwell, Connie Baumgarner, Rayo McCollough, Ruth Lawrence, Donna Peddy, Barbara York, Lara Ulrich and Georgia Ulrich all made special contributions.

Many teachers, some of whom have also been students and/or mentors, who shared the adventure of learning with me, have tested these materials and helped in their development. Some of this special group are:

Karen Crocombe
Mary Helen Livingston
Karen Van Fossen Post
Aledra Hollenbach

Sherry Bailey Owen
Eric Orr
Sue Goodman
Dr. Betty Acuff

Carol Trigg
Susan Gin
Susan Windells
Pat Dawson
Robin Kohler
Julie Harrell
Dr. Pat Webb
Mary Chaney
Michael Skobjak
Margie Flora Lundquist
Dr. Susan Zeder
Dr. Marcia Schramm Purdy
Larry Driver
Jenny Inge
Aledra Braddell
Annette Brenick
Aylette Cox
Janet Taylor
Mickey Fischer
Kathleen Denman
Polly Walton

Francine Brown
Elaine Ward
Rozelle Kessner
Marilyn Rice
Jim Harrell
Rhoda Harrell Reynolds
Dr. Don Cox
Michael McCann
Linda Johns
Deveraux Swanson Carter
Dr. Charles Helfert
Dr. Dorthy Pierce
Donna Boyd
Wally Linebarger
Ellie Caston
Candance Birk
Laura Allard
Cinda Thoma
Davida Weiss
Deborah Riddles Hanschen
John Paul Thompson

I also wish to acknowledge the stimulating influence of a special book, DESIGN YOURSELF, by Hanks, Belliston and Edwards. This book was a primary catalyst toward my decision to self-publish and do my own illustrations and lay-out. It has been a model for the visual presentation of my book and I am especially grateful for the inspiration and vision which came from DESIGN YOURSELF.

Finally, I wish to thank my husband and friend, Larry Cooper, for making my time free to work on this project and for providing constant encouragement and a strong belief in what I had to contribute. To all these people I express my sincere thanks.

CONTENTS

Characteristics of Creative Thinking

11 Assumptions Guaranteed to Block Creativity

Conceptual Repatterning

Developing PO Power

Vocabulary Through the Right Brain

Bloom's Taxonomy

Guilford's Structure of Intellect

Designing a Brain Power Center

Glossary

Further Resoures

About the Author

OVERVIEW

why
THIS BOOK WAS WRITTEN...

IN TRADITIONAL EDUCATION SO MUCH OF THE BRAIN IS LEFT UNDERDEVELOPED AND UNAPPRECIATED. DR. J. PAUL GUILFORD, WHO IN TWO DECADES OF RESEARCH DEVELOPED THE STRUCTURE OF INTELLECT (NOW KNOWN AS S.O.I.) NOTES THAT TRADITIONAL EDUCATION DEVELOPS AND REWARDS APPROXIMATELY 12 OF 120 TYPES OF HUMAN POTENTIAL. I.Q. TESTS MEASURE ONLY EIGHT OF THESE 120 TYPES, BY SOME ESTIMATIONS, AND THE AVERAGE OF THIS SMALL SAMPLING OF INTELLECTUAL POTENTIAL BECOMES THE I.Q. SCORE. WHAT A WASTE TO IGNORE PERHAPS AS MUCH AS 90% OF THE BRAIN'S TOTAL POTENTIAL! AND HOW MISLEADING TO USE A SCORE FOR MEASURING INTELLIGENCE THAT OVERLOOKS SUCH A HIGH PERCENTAGE OF THE BRAIN'S TOTAL POTENTIAL.

who...

THIS BOOK IS DESIGNED TO ASSIST ANYONE INTERESTED IN BUILDING BRAIN POWER BY EXPANDING AWARENESS OF AND THE ABILITY TO APPLY MORE OF THE BRAIN'S CAPACITY. THE THEORIES AND BRAIN BUILDERS (ACTIVITIES) HAVE BEEN WIDELY TESTED WITH KINDERGARTEN THROUGH POST-DOCTORAL STUDENTS IN BOTH PUBLIC AND PRIVATE SCHOOLS ACROSS THE COUNTRY AND WITH STUDENTS IN ADVANCED TECHNOLOGY AND CHURCH SCHOOLS, EXECUTIVES IN BUSINESS AND INDUSTRY, AND CLIENTS IN HOSPITAL THERAPY PROGRAMS. THE THEORIES AND ACTIVITIES HAVE BEEN ESPECIALLY VALUABLE TO THE PUBLIC SCHOOL TEACHER STRUGGLING WITH BURNOUT (OR LOSS OF JOY AND PROFESSIONAL FULFILLMENT) AND HAVE ENRICHED AND STRENGTHENED THE EDUCATIONAL PROGRAM AT ALL LEVELS WHILE INCREASING THE ENTHUSIASM FOR LEARNING IN BOTH TEACHER AND STUDENT.

THERE IS A GROWING AWARENESS OF THE WASTED RESOURCES OF GIFTED MINDS AND, AS A RESULT, MORE AND MORE COMMUNITIES ARE DEVELOPING PROGRAMS TO CHALLENGE AND STIMULATE THE GIFTED STUDENT. THE CONTENTS OF THIS BOOK HAVE BEEN USED SUCCESSFULLY WITH ADMINISTRATORS, PARENTS OF THE GIFTED, TEACHERS RECEIVING GRADUATE TRAINING IN EDUCATION FOR THE GIFTED, AS WELL AS WITH STUDENTS IDENTIFIED AS GIFTED FROM KINDERGARTEN THROUGH GRADE TWELVE. A MAJOR EMPHASIS OF THIS BOOK IS TO PROVIDE ANY PARENT OR TEACHER WITH A RICH RESOURCE FOR CHALLENGING AND DEVELOPING THE GIFTED DIMENSION OF ONE OR MORE STUDENTS WITH MIXED ABILITY.

what...

THIS BOOK PRESENTS A SEQUENTIAL DEVELOPMENT OF IDEAS AND SKILLS THAT, WHEN APPLIED, EXPAND THE DEVELOPMENT AND CAPACITY OF THE HUMAN BRAIN. AS NOTED IN THE TABLE OF CONTENTS, EACH SECTION PRESENTS A KEY IDEA WHICH WILL BE LISTED IN THE UPPER RIGHT CORNER OF THE PAGES IN THAT SECTION. ALTHOUGH EACH IDEA IS PRESENTED IN A BRIEF SUMMARY FOR QUICK ASSIMILATION BY THE READER, REFERENCES TO MORE IN-DEPTH INFORMATION CAN BE FOUND IN THE FURTHER RESOURCES SECTION.

FOLLOWING THE DISCUSSION OF EACH IDEA WILL BE ONE OR MORE BRAIN BUILDER ACTIVITIES DESIGNED TO APPLY THAT THEORY. ALTHOUGH EACH BRAIN BUILDER USES ALL THE SKILLS TAUGHT IN THIS BOOK, A FEW BRAIN BUILDERS ARE CHOSEN SPECIFICALLY FOR EACH SECTION TO EXERCISE THAT SPECIFIC SKILL. BRAIN BUILDERS ARE HAND LETTERED TO MAKE THEM EASY TO SPOT. THESE ARE DELIGHTFUL, ZANY IDEAS WHICH CHALLENGE THE MIND TO GROW IN NEW DIRECTIONS. ONE OF THE PRIMARY VALUES OF THIS BOOK IS THAT IT GIVES LEGITIMATE EDUCATIONAL RATIONALE FOR USING THE MARVELOUS, PLAYFUL IDEAS MANY TEACHERS HAVE INTUITIVELY BOOTLEGGED INTO THEIR TEACHING WITHOUT REALIZING THEIR INTRINSIC VALUE.

A CHALLENGING GROUP OF POSTERS AND VISUALS CAN GREATLY STRENGTHEN AND ENHANCE LEARNING SINCE WE LEARN THROUGH ALL OUR SENSES. IT IS IMPORTANT TO NOTE THAT EACH PERSON HAS A PERSONAL LEARNING PATTERN; SOME PEOPLE ARE VISUAL LEARNERS, SOME VERBAL LEARNERS, SOME KINESTHETIC LEARNERS, ETC. ACTIVITIES SUCH AS DAYDREAMING AND THE USE OF HUMOR AND PLAY HAVE BEEN FOUND TO BE IMPORTANT METHODS OF BUILDING INTELLIGENCE AND BRAIN POWER. THE POSTERS SUGGESTED IN THIS BOOK CAN SERVE AS REMINDERS TO BOTH THE TEACHER AND THE STUDENT HOW AND WHY THE EXERCISES ARE USED TO ENRICH THE CURRICULUM.

THROUGH-OUT THIS BOOK YOU WILL FIND

suggestions

for posters
stressing
Key ideas

THE SURROUNDING BORDER IS YOUR KEY TO A POSSIBLE POSTER IDEA. INVITE A STUDENT TO ENLARGE THE IDEA AND LINK NEW IDEAS OF THEIR OWN INTO THE IMAGES, COLORS AND LETTERING THEY USE.

how...

THIS BOOK CAN BE USED SEQUENTIALLY AS A SEPARATE SECTION OF THE CURRICULUM OR TO ENHANCE AND ENRICH THE TOTAL CURRICULUM. FOR TEACHERS THE EDUCATIONAL THEORIES (RATIONALE) ARE PRESENTED, FOLLOWED BY SUGGESTED POSTER IDEAS WHICH MIGHT BE USED AS OVERHEAD TRANSPARENCIES, POSTERS IN THE CLASSROOM, ON TAKE-HOME MATERIAL FOR PARENTS OR AS OTHER LEARNING REINFORCEMENT.

THE BRAIN BUILDER PAGES (ALL HAND LETTERED) CAN BE CUT OUT AND LAMINATED, USED AS SPECIAL INTEREST CENTERS, INDIVIDUAL OR SMALL GROUP ACTIVITIES TO CHALLENGE FASTER STUDENTS WITH MORE DIVERSE THINKING, OR AS ACTIVITIES FOR THE TOTAL CLASS. LINKS TO THE WHOLE CURRICULUM ARE NOTED ON THE REVERSE SIDE OF EACH BRAIN BUILDER.

A **Glossary** OF SPECIAL TERMS CAN BE FOUND AT THE BACK OF THE BOOK FOLLOWED BY A **Further Resource** SECTION. THIS INCLUDES READINGS AND OTHER MATERIALS TO GIVE GREATER DEPTH TO MANY OF THE IDEAS AND THEORIES PRESENTED IN SUMMARY.

one final note...

AT THE HEART OF THESE MANY TEACHING IDEAS IS THE DEVELOPMENT OF *creativity* AS A LIFE RESOURCE FOR PROBLEM-SOLVING, INVENTING, DESIGNING AND DECISION MAKING SKILLS. STRENGTH AND AGILITY IN CREATIVE THINKING REQUIRES TIME AND EFFORT. IF, AT FIRST, IT SEEMS AWKWARD AND DIFFICULT TO GET CREATIVITY FLOWING, THINK ABOUT THE FOLLOWING ANALOGY. IF A STRONG, WELL DEVELOPED RUNNER BREAKS A LEG AND HAS IT IMMOBILIZED IN A CAST FOR SEVERAL WEEKS, WHEN THE CAST IS REMOVED THE MUSCLES HAVE ATROPHIED OR WITHERED. THE LEG IS SMALLER THAN THE HEALTHY LEG AND RETURNING IT TO TOP CONDITION IS A SLOW, AWKWARD AND SOMETIMES PAINFULLY DIS-COURAGING PROCESS.

IN THE SAME WAY, IF CREATIVE THINKING HAS BEEN SET ASIDE FOR SEVERAL MONTHS OR YEARS, IT WILL HAVE WITHERED FROM LACK OF USE. TO GET IT STRONG, AGILE, AND PRODUCTIVE AGAIN WILL TAKE PATIENCE, TIME AND PRACTICE. THE BRAIN BUILDERS IN THIS BOOK ARE DESIGNED TO DEVELOP A STRONG, HEALTHY, CREATIVE MENTAL PROCESS. THE MANY CREATIVE IDEA STARTERS GIVEN WITH EACH BRAIN BRUILDER ARE IMBEDDED AS "PUMP-PRIMERS" TO GET THE CREATIVE JUICES FLOWING. SO ADD YOUR OWN IDEAS AND ENCOURAGE YOURSELF AND STUDENTS TO

ALWAYS

TAKE THE IDEAS FARTHER.

THE MOST IMPORTANT POINT IS TO UNLEASH YOUR OWN ORIGINAL THINKING. LET IT OUT. LET IT GROW. GIVEN TIME, EXERCISE AND APPRECIATION ANYONE CAN REGAIN THE HIGH LEVEL OF CREATIVITY ONCE ACTIVE IN EARLY CHILDHOOD.

IN TEACHING FOR CREATIVE THINKING ONE OF THE MOST EFFECTIVE STRATEGIES IS TO BE

AN ACTIVE ROLE MODEL OF CREATIVE THINKING.

BE INVOLVED IN THE PROCESS. SOON YOU WILL FIND THAT YOUR OWN ORIGINAL CREATIVE IDEAS WILL BE STIMULATED. TAKE OFF FROM THE BRAIN BUILDERS. THINK UP YOUR OWN. ENCOURAGE YOUR STUDENTS TO DO THE SAME. ONE MEASURE OF HOW EFFECTIVE THIS BOOK IS COULD BE HOW MUCH YOU, THE READER, BEGIN TO DEVIATE FROM THE CONTENT. IF YOU HAVE SOME FAVORITES YOU WOULD LIKE TO SHARE WITH THE AUTHOR, I'D BE EAGER TO RECEIVE THEM THROUGH THE FOLLOWING ADDRESS:

DR. ANN MCGEE-COOPER
4236 HOCKADAY
DALLAS, TEXAS 75229

RIGHT HEMISPHERE	LEFT HEMISPHERE
IRRATIONAL	RATIONAL
ILLOGICAL	LOGICAL
HOLISTIC	LINEAR
SPONTANEOUS	SEQUENTIAL
FEELINGS	FACTS
IMAGINATION	KNOWLEDGE
ART, MUSIC, DANCE, MIME, THEATRE	LANGUAGE, MATH, LAW
INTUITION	SYSTEMS, RULES
SPATIAL	SYMBOLS
PEOPLE-ORIENTED	FACT-ORIENTED
"LET'S DO IT!"	"LET'S PLAN FIRST!"
CREATIVE	IMPLEMENT
THINK IN PICTURES	THINK IN WORDS AND FIGURES
DREAMER, PLAYFUL	WORKER, SERIOUS
3-D THINKING	2-D THINKING

CORPUS callosum

Double Your Brain Power: The Importance of Balancing Brain Development

RECENT RESEARCH GIVES US STRONG EVIDENCE THAT TRADITIONAL EDUCATION TURNS ITS BACK ON, DISCOUNTS, OR LEAVES AS UNWORTHY OF DEVELOPMENT AT LEAST HALF OF THE BRAIN. TO UNDERSTAND THIS MORE FULLY, LET'S LOOK AT THE THEORIES THAT ARISE FROM RESEARCH ON THE SPLIT BRAIN.

APPROXIMATELY TWENTY-FIVE YEARS AGO, RESEARCH BEGAN WHICH LED TO THE DISCOVERY THAT EACH HEMISPHERE OF THE BRAIN PERFORMS RADICALLY DIFFERENT TASKS. IT IS ALMOST LIKE HAVING TWO VERY DIFFERENT BRAINS. THE RIGHT AND THE LEFT HEMISPHERE CAN WORK ON THE SAME PROBLEM BUT WILL USE OPPOSITE PROCESSES IN COMING TO A SOLUTION.

CONNECTING THESE HEMISPHERES IS A BUNDLE OF NERVE FIBERS CALLED THE CORPUS CALLOSUM. THESE SERVE LIKE A HIGHLY EFFICIENT TELEPHONE CABLE OR AS A MESSAGE HIGHWAY CONNECTING THE THINKING OF BOTH SIDES OF THE BRAIN. THOUGHTS RACE BACK AND FORTH ACROSS THE CORPUS CALLOSUM AS WE CONSTANTLY DRAW FROM BOTH SIDES OF OUR BRAIN TO SOLVE DAILY PROBLEMS.

LET'S LOOK AT THE FUNCTION OF EACH SIDE OF THE BRAIN. (SEE ILLUSTRATION ON OPPOSITE PAGE.)

DURING THE FIRST FIVE YEARS OF LIFE, WE ALL OPERATE PRIMARILY FROM OUR RIGHT HEMISPHERE. THIS IS THE HOME OF FANTASY, MAKE-BELIEVE, CREATIVITY, FEELINGS AND PLAYFULNESS. LOGIC IS DORMANT WHILE WE FROLIC WITH OUR IMAGINATION. WE ARE SPONTANEOUS, MOVE QUICKLY FROM ONE INTEREST TO ANOTHER, RELATE MORE TO PICTURES AND ACTION THAN TO WORDS.

THEN AT APPROXIMATELY AGE SIX WE ENTER SCHOOL AND BEGIN DEVELOPING OUR LEFT HEMISPHERE. NOW WE LEARN RULES, ORDER, LINEAR SEQUENCING.

A, B, C, D . . . 1, 2, 3, 4 . . . "FIRST WE SAY THE PLEDGE OF ALLEGIANCE, THEN WE READ AND THEN WE HAVE RECESS ..."

WE BEGIN TO LEARN ABOUT LOGIC, FACTS, LANGUAGE AND MATH (WHICH ARE SYSTEMS AND SYMBOLS). WE LEAVE BEHIND THE STRONG POTENTIAL OF OUR RIGHT BRAIN EXCEPT FOR ART AND RECESS, WHICH WE SOON LEARN ARE JUST FOR FUN AND NOT NEARLY AS IMPORTANT AS READING AND WRITING. WHEN WE ANSWER QUESTIONS BASED ON OUR INTUITION (KNOWING WITHOUT KNOWING THE BASIS OR RATIONAL FOR OUR KNOWING) WE ARE OFTEN TOLD THAT WE ARE WRONG OR EVEN CHEATING. IF WE DON'T KNOW HOW WE KNOW, THAT IS OFTEN SEEN AS BEING AS BAD AS NOT KNOWING.

DAY BY DAY WE BEGIN TO DISCOUNT RIGHT BRAIN PROCESSES IN FAVOR OF THE LEFT BRAIN. LOOK BACK AT THE DIAGRAM OF THE RIGHT/LEFT HEMISPHERES. DO YOU SEE ANY WORDS THAT ARE USED TO PUT DOWN A PERSON OR IDEA?

HAVE YOU HEARD ANYONE RIDICULED FOR BEING
IRRATIONAL, ILLOGICAL OR HAVING HIS/HER HEAD
IN THE CLOUDS (DREAMING)? MANY TIMES WHEN A
PERSON WORKS HOLISTICALLY WE CALL THEM SCATTERED
OR SCATTER-BRAINED. THE ABSENTMINDED PERSON IS
USUALLY FOCUSED HEAVILY ON RIGHT-BRAINED THINK-
ING (CREATIVITY, WOOL GATHERING, DAY DREAMING)
AND NOT AT ALL FOCUSED ON LEFT-BRAINED THINKING
(BEING ON TIME, BEING GOAL-ORIENTED). WHEN WE
REALIZE THAT WE HAVE INHERITED A VALUE SYSTEM
THAT PLACES SUCH LOW VALUE ON HALF OUR BRAIN
POWER, IS IT ANY WONDER THAT WE USE SO LITTLE
OF OUR BRAIN? ONLY THOSE PEOPLE WITH THE INNER
COURAGE TO IGNORE THE OPINIONS AND PREJUDICE
OF THE MAJORITY OF SOCIETY HAVE THE OPTION OF
HARVESTING 50% OF THE BRAIN POWER THAT THE REST
OF US MAKE JOKES ABOUT AND OVERLOOK.

IT IS INTERESTING TO NOTE THAT PEOPLE IN
THE WESTERN HEMISPHERE PLACE A HIGH VALUE ON
LEFT-BRAINED PROCESSES AND DISCOUNT THE RIGHT
BRAIN, WHILE THE REVERSE IS TRUE HALF WAY
ROUND THE WORLD. IN TRADITIONAL CHINA, INDIA
AND JAPAN A HIGH VALUE IS PLACED ON AESTHETICS,
SENSITIVITY TO PEOPLE'S FEELINGS, THE HOLISTIC
INTEGRATION OF FAMILY, RELIGION, WORK AND SCHOOL,
WHILE SUCH CONCERNS AS BEING PROMPT AND LOGICAL
ARE SEEN AS TRITE AND FAR LESS IMPORTANT. IS
IT ANY WONDER THAT WE ARE HAVING TROUBLE IN
INTERNATIONAL AFFAIRS WHEN BASIC VALUES ARE SO
DIFFERENT?

IT SHOULD BE NOTED THAT THE LOSS ALSO
OCCURS WHEN RIGHT-BRAINED THINKERS PUT DOWN
LEFT-BRAINED THINKERS WITH COMMENTS SUCH AS,

"HE'S SO BORING AND UNIMAGINATIVE!"
OR "ALL SHE THINKS OF IS THE BOTTOM
LINE. SUCH A LACK OF VISION ... SHE'S
SO MYOPIC!" OR "HE'S IN SUCH A RUT...
SAME THING FOR BREAKFAST, LUNCH AND

SUPPER. IT'S TUESDAY, HE'S WEARING HIS BLUE STRIPED SUIT. HO-HUM."

AS LONG AS WE LIMIT OURSELVES TO VALUING ONLY ONE SIDE OF THE BRAIN NO MATTER WHICH SIDE WE PREFER, WE ARE ONLY PUTTING 50% OF OUR POTENTIAL TO WORK. AN ENORMOUS NEW CAPACITY CAN BE OURS SIMPLY BY LEARNING TO VALUE BOTH SIDES OF THE BRAIN EQUALLY AND LEARNING TO BRING THEM BOTH INTO PLAY SIMULTANEOUSLY.

SOMEWHERE IN THE GROWING-UP YEARS EACH PERSON SEEMS TO ESTABLISH A DOMINANT BRAIN HEMISPHERE WHICH IS CALLED UPON MOST OFTEN. JUST AS WE EACH SEEM TO UNCONSCIOUSLY ESTABLISH A HAND DOMINANCE AND BECOME LEFT-HANDED OR RIGHT-HANDED, SO DO WE EACH SEEM TO ESTABLISH A BRAIN DOMINANCE. EVEN THOUGH WE ALL USE BOTH SIDES OF OUR BRAINS SIMULTANEOUSLY AND CONSTANTLY, MOST OF US GRAVITATE TO BEING MOST COMFORTABLE, MORE AT HOME WITH A PREFERRED SIDE OF OUR BRAIN. THIS WILL BE REFERRED TO AS BEING LEFT-BRAINED OR RIGHT-BRAINED. IT IS TRUE THAT SOME PEOPLE DO LEARN TO BE WHOLE-BRAINED OR TO CALL EQUALLY ON BOTH SIDES OF THEIR BRAIN AS APPROPRIATE TO THEIR NEEDS. THIS, IN FACT, IS THE PREFERRED LEVEL OF ABILITY TO ATTAIN. EACH OF US CAN GAIN A FAR GREATER PERSONAL POTENTIAL BY LEARNING TO CALL EQUALLY ON BOTH SIDES OF OUR BRAIN. THIS IS MY PURPOSE IN DISCUSSING SPLIT BRAIN AND BRAIN DOMINANCE.

IF WE DID NOTHING MORE THAN TO BALANCE THE APPRECIATION

AND DEVELOPMENT OF BOTH SIDES OF THE BRAIN, WE COULD MORE

THAN DOUBLE THE POTENTIAL OF EACH STUDENT AND OF OURSELVES!

WHAT IS YOUR BRAIN-DOMINANCE PATTERN?

ARE YOU CURIOUS ABOUT WHICH SIDE OF YOUR BRAIN IS DOMINANT? THE FOLLOWING SELF-TEST IS DESIGNED TO GIVE YOU SOME INSIGHTS INTO YOUR OWN PATTERN OF BRAIN DOMINANCE. IT IS DESIGNED PRIMARILY FOR YOUNGSTERS THOUGH ADULTS CAN USE IT TOO BY SIMPLY MAKING IT FIT THE SITUATIONS OF ADULT LIFE.

FOR EACH OF THE FOLLOWING EXAMPLES, RATE YOURSELF ON A SCALE OF 1 TO 5 BEING MOST RIGHT-BRAINED OR LEFT-BRAINED AND 0 BEING A BALANCE BETWEEN THE TWO.

TYPICAL LEFT-BRAIN BEHAVIOR

TYPICAL RIGHT-BRAIN BEHAVIOR

1. THINK OF YOUR BEDROOM AS IT USUALLY IS OR AS YOU PREFER IT TO BE. IS IT NEAT AND ORDERLY, A PLACE FOR EACH THING AND EACH THING IN ITS PLACE?

OR IS IT CLUTTER AND CHAOS WITH THE IDEA THAT "SOMEDAY I'LL GET ORGANIZED?"

(Now rate your typical behavior on the following scale. Circle the number that represents your preferred typical behavior.)

5   4   3   2   1   0   1   2   3   4   5

2. THINK OF YOUR DESK AT SCHOOL OR YOUR LOCKER. IS IT USUALLY NEAT AND ORDERLY?

OR DO YOU USUALLY JUST PILE THINGS IN AND DIG AROUND FOR WHAT YOU NEED?

5   4   3   2   1   0   1   2   3   4   5

3. DO YOU FEEL MOST COMFORTABLE WHEN YOU HAVE DINNER AT THE SAME TIME EACH DAY?

OR DO YOU PREFER TO EAT WHEN YOU GET HUNGRY...MAYBE AT 5:00 ONE EVENING AND AT 8:00 THE NEXT?

5   4   3   2   1   0   1   2   3   4   5

4. DO YOU PREFER TO WORK CROSSWORD PUZZLES, PLAY CHECKERS OR CHESS, READ BOOKS?

OR DO YOU PREFER TO RIDE YOUR BICYCLE, PLAY BALL, FLY KITES, DRAW PICTURES OR WORK IN CLAY?

(IF YOUR ANSWER IS SOME OF EACH THEN CIRCLE A NUMBER CLOSE TO THE MIDDLE.)

5   4   3   2   1   0   1   2   3   4   5

5. DO YOU USUALLY PREFER TO STUDY WITH NO DISTRACTIONS? DO YOU CLOSE THE DOOR AND LIKE QUIET? DO YOU LIKE TO WORK UNTIL YOU FINISH, LONG PERIODS WITH FEW BREAKS TO GET THE WORK DONE?

OR DO YOU LIKE TO TURN ON SOME BACKGROUND MUSIC, BUILD A YUMMY SANDWICH, TAKE FREQUENT BREAKS, CHANGE YOUR POSITION FROM SITTING TO LYING ON THE FLOOR TO FEET PROPPED UP ON A CHAIR?

5   4   3   2   1   0   1   2   3   4   5

6. DO YOU PREFER TO COMPLETE ONE TASK OR GAME AND PUT IT AWAY BE-FORE YOU BEGIN THE NEXT? (OR FINISH READING ONE BOOK OR MAGAZINE BEFORE YOU OPEN ANOTHER?)

OR ARE YOU IN THE MIDDLE OF READ-ING SEVERAL BOOKS AND MAGAZINES AT ONCE? OR DO YOU TYPICALLY GET SEVERAL ACTIVITIES GOING AT ONCE? MAYBE YOU GET OUT A GAME AND WHILE YOU ARE SETTING IT UP YOU SEE SOMETHING ELSE YOU DECIDE TO DO AND THEN YOU HEAR SOMEONE OUTSIDE AND SO YOU GRAB YOUR SWEATER AND GO OUT FOR AWHILE?

5   4   3   2   1   0   1   2   3   4   5

7. DO YOU LIKE TO STICK TO THE SAME FAVORITE FOODS?

OR DO YOU ENJOY TRYING OUT NEW FOODS, NEW FLAVORS OF ICE CREAM, NEW VEGETABLES, NEW RESTAURANTS AND RECIPES?

5   4   3   2   1   0   1   2   3   4   5

8. DO YOU ALWAYS TAKE THE SAME ROUTE HOME OR TO SCHOOL?

OR DO YOU SOMETIMES OR OFTEN CHOOSE TO GO HOME A NEW WAY JUST TO BREAK UP THE MONOTONY?

5   4   3   2   1   0   1   2   3   4   5

9. HOW CREATIVELY DO YOU USE FREE TIME? ARE SUNDAYS THE SAME OVER AND OVER? DO YOU WATCH THE SAME CARTOONS EVERY SATURDAY, PLAY WITH THE SAME FRIENDS?

OR DO YOU SEARCH FOR NEW IDEAS, NEW PROJECTS, NEW FRIENDS, NEW ACTIVITIES?

5   4   3   2   1   0   1   2   3   4   5

10. DO YOU ALWAYS WATCH THE SAME PROGRAMS OR VIEW TV AT THE SAME TIME EACH DAY?

OR DO YOU CHECK THE TV GUIDE TO FIND NEW, INTERESTING OPTIONS? DO YOU LIKE TO PLAY A GAME OR DO SOMETHING ELSE WHILE YOU WATCH TV?

5   4   3   2   1   0   1   2   3   4   5

11. IF YOU WERE MOVING TO A NEW HOUSE WOULD YOU PREFER TO MAKE A DIAGRAM OF YOUR NEW ROOM AND DRAW A FLOOR PLAN OF WHAT WOULD FIT WHERE?

OR WOULD YOU RATHER JUST WAIT UNTIL YOU GET THERE AND MOVE THINGS AROUND UNTIL THEY LOOK RIGHT? (IF YOU IMAGINE THINGS IN YOUR MIND SPATIALLY TO PLAN WHERE TO PUT THEM, THIS IS ALSO RIGHT-BRAINED.)

5   4   3   2   1   0   1   2   3   4   5

14

NOW TOTAL YOUR SCORES AND SEE WHAT YOUR
PROFILE LOOKS LIKE. DO YOU HAVE EXTREME RIGHT-
BRAIN AND EXTREME LEFT-BRAIN RESPONSES? ARE
MOST OF YOUR ANSWERS SOMEWHERE IN THE MIDDLE?
ARE YOU MOSTLY ON ONE SIDE? REMEMBER, THERE IS
NO RIGHT ANSWER OR BEST PROFILE. WHATEVER YOUR
PROFILE MAY BE, IT IS IMPORTANT TO UNDERSTAND
AND PLACE A HIGH VALUE ON YOUR DOMINANCE OR PRE-
FERRED BEHAVIOR. THEN YOU CAN BUILD ON YOUR
STRENGTHS IN TWO WAYS.

1. LEARN THE VALUE OF EACH SIDE OF THE
BRAIN AND HAVE A SINCERE APPRECIATION FOR EACH
DOMINANCE. WE LOSE VALUABLE ENERGY BY FEELING
GUILTY OR INADEQUATE. WE CAN BUILD OUR ENERGY
AND MOTIVATION BY INCREASING OUR UNDERSTANDING
AND APPRECIATION FOR OUR NATURAL STRENGTHS.

2. LEARN HOW TO BALANCE YOUR PROFILE.
CHOOSE TO WORK AND PLAY WITH OTHERS WHO HAVE
OPPOSITE STRENGTHS BUT BE SURE THAT EACH OF YOU
APPRECIATES THE OTHER'S STRENGTHS. IF YOU ARE
COMPETING TO SEE WHICH WAY IS BEST, YOU WILL LOSE
ENERGY AND POTENTIAL. EACH SIDE OF THE BRAIN
MAKES A VALUABLE CONTRIBUTION. HOWEVER, A WHOLE-
BRAIN APPROACH WILL ALWAYS BRING MORE POTENTIAL
TO ANY PROBLEM OR PROJECT. YOU CAN CONTINUALLY
STRENGTHEN YOUR WEAKER SIDE OF THE BRAIN BY OFTEN
WORKING AND PLAYING WITH OTHERS WHO HAVE THE
OPPOSITE BRAIN DOMINANCE.

IT IS IMPORTANT TO NOTE THAT THE CONDITIONS
WHICH ENERGIZE ONE SIDE OF THE BRAIN, FRUSTRATE
AND DRAIN THE OTHER SIDE OF THE BRAIN. FOR
EXAMPLE, THE LEFT-BRAIN PREFERS ORDER, PLANNING,
ORGANIZATION, AN ABSENCE OF CLUTTER, FINISHING
ONE TASK BEFORE BEGINNING ANOTHER. THIS PROCESS
AND ENVIRONMENT TIRES AND BORES A GIFTED OR

DOMINANT RIGHT-BRAIN PERSON WHO WILL THRIVE ON:

- WORKING ON SEVERAL TASKS SIMULTANEOUSLY
  (IDEAS FROM ONE TASK LINK CREATIVELY TO
  IDEAS FROM ANOTHER)

- ABUNDANCE OF SENSORY STIMULATION (THE
  LEFT-BRAIN WOULD CALL THIS CLUTTER,
  NOISE, DISTRACTIONS)

- SPONTANEOUS INTERACTION WITH OTHERS.

A GIFTED OR DOMINANT LEFT-BRAIN PERSON WOULD FIND IT DIFFICULT INDEED TO SURVIVE, MUCH LESS THRIVE, IN THE TYPICAL RIGHT-BRAIN HAVEN OF COMFORT. REMEMBER, THE CONDITIONS WHICH NURTURE THE MOST SUCCESSFUL WORKING ENVIRONMENT FOR A PERSON DOMINANT IN ONE SIDE OF THE BRAIN WILL TIRE AND FRUSTRATE ANOTHER PERSON WHO IS DOMINANT IN THE OPPOSITE SIDE OF THE BRAIN. AS TEACHERS AND PARENTS, WE NEED TO DESIGN WORKING/ LEARNING ENVIRONMENTS WHICH HAVE CONDITIONS TO NURTURE AND SUPPORT THE POSITIVE DEVELOPMENT OF BOTH SIDES OF THE BRAIN. THIS IS INDEED A CHALLENGE.

IT WILL GREATLY IMPROVE OUR PERSONAL PRODUCTIVITY IF WE CAN UNDERSTAND AND PROVIDE FOR OURSELF THOSE CONDITIONS WHICH ENHANCE OUR OWN PERSONAL PATTERN OF BRAIN DOMINANCE. BUT WE ALSO NEED TO CONTINUALLY EXPAND OUR TOLERANCE FOR WORKING PRODUCTIVELY IN AN ENVIRONMENT THAT IS OPPOSITE TO OUR PREFERENCE, BOTH TO INCREASE OUR LESS DOMINANT TRAITS AND TO BE ABLE TO WORK EFFECTIVELY WITH OTHERS DIFFERENT FROM OURSELVES.

16

ALBERT EINSTEIN STARTLED MANY PEOPLE ON
RECEIVING AN AWARD AT THE HEIGHT OF HIS CAREER
BY SAYING,

"IMAGINATION IS MORE IMPORTANT THAN KNOWLEDGE,

FOR KNOWLEDGE IS LIMITED (to all we now know and understand)

WHILE IMAGINATION EMBRACES THE ENTIRE WORLD (and all

there ever will be to know and understand)."

EINSTEIN WAS KEENLY AWARE OF THE VAST,
OVERLOOKED POTENTIAL OF THE RIGHT BRAIN. SO
WAS DR. E. PAUL TORRANCE WHOSE RESEARCH HAS
CONTRIBUTED SO MUCH TO OUR UNDERSTANDING OF
CREATIVE PROBLEM SOLVING. TORRANCE TELLS US
THAT OFTEN THE SEEDS OF A POTENTIALLY HIGHLY
SIGNIFICANT IDEA HIDE IN WHAT SEEMS TO BE THE
MOST OUTRAGEOUS IDEA...ONE WE MIGHT CALL JUST
PLAIN NONSENSE.

BOTH OF THESE MEN HAVE A HIGH REGARD FOR
THE IMPORTANT PART THE RIGHT HEMISPHERE PLAYS
IN THE CREATIVE PROCESS. THINK OF THE RIGHT
BRAIN OR THE IMAGINATION AS BEING A SORT OF
BUTTERFLY NET USED TO CAPTURE HIGHLY CREATIVE
IDEAS. REMEMBER THAT EVERY NEW IDEA THAT IS
HIGHLY CREATIVE SEEMED VERY STRANGE, EVEN
CRAZY ON FIRST GLANCE. SO EXPECT TO FEEL THE
SAME WAY ABOUT YOUR NEWEST IDEAS SNAGGED IN
THE NET OF YOUR IMAGINATION. YOU WILL PROBABLY
THINK THEY ARE "JUST FOR FUN!" BUT REALIZE
THAT, ONCE CAPTURED, THESE PRODUCTS OF OUR
IMAGINATION ARE BROUGHT OUT TO ANALYZE (LEFT-
BRAIN), REFINE, ADJUST, POLISH...AND FINALLY
EXPLAIN TO OTHERS. ONCE WE CAN EXPLAIN A NEW

IDEA IT MOVES FROM BEING PURE IMAGINATION TO BEING KNOWLEDGE (SOMETHING WE CAN UNDERSTAND AND EXPLAIN). IT TOOK SEVERAL YEARS BETWEEN THE TIME EINSTEIN FIRST GOT THE IDEA FOR HIS THEORY OF RELATIVITY (imagination) UNTIL HE COULD EXPLAIN IT TO OTHERS (knowledge).

MOST OF US MAKE THE MISTAKE OF EXPECTING OUR NEW IDEAS TO ARRIVE WITH ALL THE DIGNITY AND RECOGNIZED MERIT OF IDEAS THAT HAVE BEEN AROUND LONG ENOUGH TO BE CONSIDERED KNOWLEDGE. JUST REMEMBER THAT THE INFANCY OF ALL KNOW-LEDGE IS CALLED IMAGINATION...AND OFTEN IT IS ALSO CALLED WEIRD, CRAZY, RIDICULOUS AND OUTRAGEOUS. DON'T LET YOUR BEST IDEAS GET CAST ASIDE OR LEFT UNDISCOVERED BECAUSE THEY FRIGHTEN YOU WITH THEIR OUTRAGEOUSNESS FOR SUCH ARE THE CLOTHES OF NEW DISCOVERIES.

IT IS IMPORTANT TO UNDERSTAND THAT SCHOOLS NEED NOT BLOCK THE CONTINUING GROWTH OF THE RIGHT-BRAIN IN ORDER TO DEVELOP THE LEFT-BRAIN. IT IS A QUESTION OF BALANCE. NEITHER SIDE OF THE BRAIN IS MORE VALUABLE AND NEITHER CAN ACHIEVE SO MUCH WORKING ALONE AS EACH SIDE CAN WORKING IN TANDEM WITH THE OTHER. THIS BOOK IS DESIGNED PRIMARILY TO SHOW HOW BOTH SIDES OF THE BRAIN CAN BE NURTURED SIMULTANEOUSLY FOR A WHOLE-BRAINED PERSON TO RESULT.

PROVIDING AN ENRICHED CLIMATE FOR LEARNING

IN PLANNING TO INCREASE OUR BRAIN POWER IT IS IMPORTANT TO CHANGE TWO BASIC ATTITUDES ABOUT LEARNING. SOMEWHERE IN THE COBWEBS OF OUR BRAINS IS WRITTEN,

"LEARNING IS SERIOUS BUSINESS! WE DON'T HAVE TIME TO HORSE AROUND."

AND

"CUT OUT THE FUNNY STUFF AND GET BUSY. WE'VE HAD ENOUGH TIME FOR PLAY. LEARNING IS HARD WORK."

IT MAY BE WRITTEN IN YOUR BRAIN IN SLIGHTLY DIFFERENT WORDS AND PHRASES, BUT THE MEANING IS THE SAME.

TOO MUCH HUMOR AND TOO MUCH FUN INTERFERE WITH LEARNING.

STOP FOR A MINUTE AND CANCEL OUT THESE MESSAGES WITH A BIG X OR BETTER YET, ERASE THEM COMPLETELY. NOW REPLACE THEM WITH THE TWO MAGIC KEYS TO HIGHLY MOTIVATED LEARNING. HAVE FUN IN THE PROCESS OF LEARNING! IT OPENS YOUR MIND AND ALLOWS FOR A MORE CREATIVE FLOW OF IDEAS. WELCOME AND INCLUDE HUMOR!

IN MANY STUDIES CONCERNING HIGHER INTELLIGENCE, HUMOR IS NOTED AS A KEY FACTOR. HUMOR IS BASED ON SEEING A SITUATION FROM MORE THAN ONE POINT OF VIEW. PUNS AND DOUBLE MEANINGS HAVE THIS SAME CHARACTER-ISTIC: THEY REQUIRE FLEXIBLE INSIGHT, BROADER AND MORE COMPLEX THINKING.

THE TWO KEYS TO HIGHLY MOTIVATED LEARNING - FUN AND HUMOR - ARE ALSO ESSENTIAL IN PROGRAMS FOR GIFTED STUDENTS PRECISELY BECAUSE THEY PROMOTE

1. INTENSE AND CONCENTRATED INVOLVEMENT

2. MORE COMPLEX AND VARIED THINKING.

STRANGE AS IT MAY SEEM, THESE ARE VITAL KEYS TO

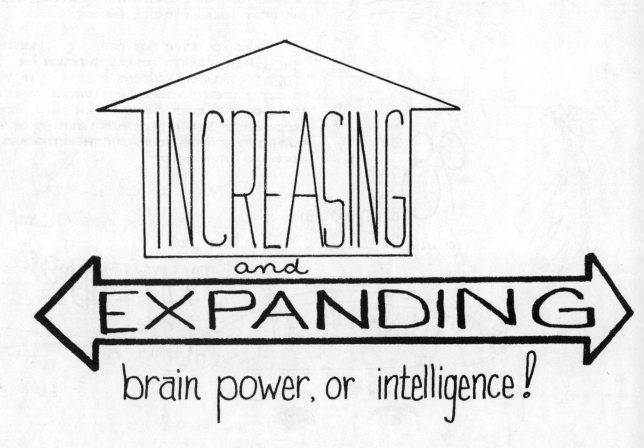

ALTHOUGH THERE IS CERTAINLY TRUTH IN THE SAYING THAT MOST CREATIVITY INVOLVES 98% PERSPIRATION AND 2% INSPIRATION, YOU MAY BE WASTING YOUR PERSPIRATION IF YOU GET BUSY WORKING BEFORE YOU HAVE TAKEN THE TIME OR MADE THE EFFORT TO PRODUCE HIGHLY CREA-TIVE OR INSPIRED IDEAS. MOST PEOPLE ARE PRONE TO ACT OFF THEIR FIRST IDEA...OR AT BEST GENERATE ONLY A FEW IDEAS BEFORE CHOOSING ONE TO PUT TO WORK FOR THEM. A HIGHLY CREATIVE PERSON KNOWS THAT IT'S USUALLY WELL WORTH THE TIME AND EFFORT TO PRODUCE MANY IDEAS, PERHAPS 68 OR 168 OR MORE, BEFORE STOP-PING TO CHOOSE THE BEST IDEA. BELOW THE LAYERS OF THE FIRST AND MORE USUAL IDEAS LAY THE FERTILE GROUND FOR THE MORE UNUSUAL, HIGHLY ORIGINAL IDEAS. JUST AS AN ATHLETE WARMS UP HIS/HER MUSCLES PRIOR TO A GAME OR PERFORMANCE, THE BRAIN NEEDS TO BE "WARMED UP" BY EXERCISING CREATIVE THINKING BEFORE THE BEST IDEAS USUALLY EMERGE.

HAVE YOU EVER NOTICED........WE USUALLY WORK MUCH HARDER TO FOLLOW THROUGH ON OUR OWN IDEAS THAN ON SOMEONE ELSE'S? IF YOUR GOAL IS TO GET STUDENTS HIGHLY MOTIVATED TO LEARN IN ALL AREAS OF THE CURRICULUM, THEN THIS BOOK IS FOR YOU! REMEMBER TO MIX A GENEROUS HELPING OF HUMOR AND PLAYFULNESS INTO YOUR OWN THINKING AND THAT OF YOUR LEARNING ENVIRONMENT.

98% perspiration
+2% inspiration

THINKING

PLAYFULNESS

HUMOR

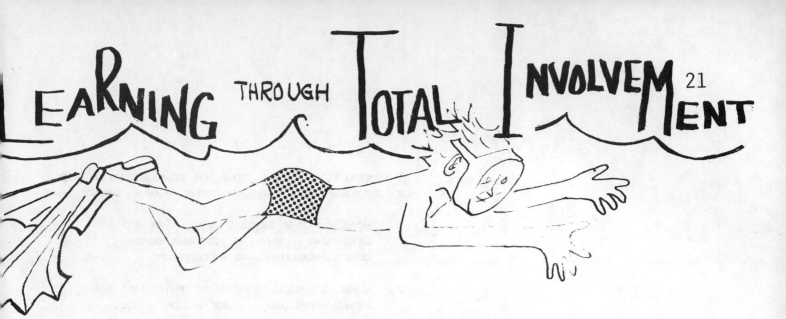

LEARNING THROUGH TOTAL INVOLVEMENT

WHEN I FIRST BEGAN USING TEACHING TECHNIQUES TO PROMOTE HIGHLY CREATIVE THINKING IN THE CLASSROOM, I HAD ADMINISTRATORS, TEACHERS AND PARENTS ASK,

"BUT WHAT ARE THEY DOING? WHY ARE THEY HAVING SO MUCH FUN? WHY AREN'T THEY IN STRAIGHT ROWS, ALL FACING THE FRONT, BOTH FEET ON THE FLOOR, I.E., LEARNING?"

AND I WOULD REPLY,

"THEY ARE LEARNING, *learning through total involvement!*"

WHEN YOU ARE HAVING FUN, AREN'T YOU TOTALLY IN-VOLVED IN WHAT YOU ARE DOING? STUDIES SHOW THAT WE RETAIN MORE IDEAS AND INFORMATION FOR LONGER PERIODS AND COMPREHEND IN GREATER DEPTH WHEN WE ARE EXPERIENCING LEARNING AND ENJOYING LEARNING.[1] JUST SUBSTITUTE "LEARNING THROUGH TOTAL INVOLVEMENT" FOR THE WORD "PLAY" AND SEE WHAT HAPPENS. AND BY ALL MEANS, BE A TOUGH JUDGE OF THE RESULTS. BUT BE OBJECTIVE.

[1] ROBERT L. STEWARD & ARTHUR D. WORKMAN, CHILDREN & OTHER PEOPLE ACHIEVING MATURITY THROUGH LEARNING, THE DRYDEN PRESS.
EDGAR DALE, AUDIOVISUAL METHODS IN TEACHING, 3RD EDITION, DRYDEN PRESS, 1969.

I PREDICT YOU WILL FIND IN YOUR EXAMINATION OF PLAY AS LEARNING THROUGH TOTAL INVOLVEMENT THAT

1. MORE OF THE SENSES ARE INVOLVED IN LEARNING. THIS HEIGHTENS BOTH COMPREHENSION AND RETENTION.

2. MORE COMPLEX LEVELS OF THINKING ARE BEING APPLIED. (SEE BLOOM'S TAX- ONOMY OF COGNITIVE THINKING, PAGE 158.)

3. MORE PLAYFUL THINKING USUALLY IN- VOLVES THE USE OF SOME OR ALL OF THE CHARACTERISTICS OF CREATIVE THINKING.

4. A LONGER AND MORE CONCENTRATED ATTENTION SPAN IS FOSTERED.

5. GREATER OPPORTUNITY TO SYNTHESIZE AND TO LINK TO OTHER AREAS OF LEARNING TAKES PLACE.

BUT PLAY LEFT UNGUIDED CAN BE A NEGLECTED GOLD MINE. AN ALERT TEACHER OR PARENT CAN GUIDE THE PLAY TO SYSTEMATICALLY

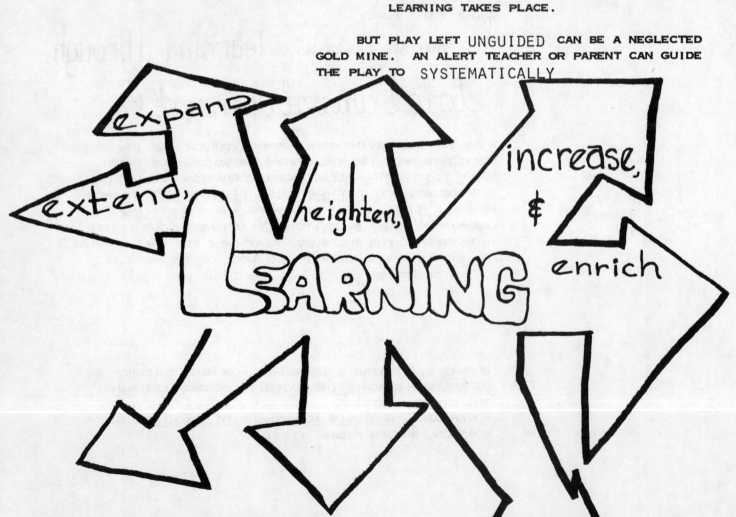

JEROME S. BRUNER IN AN ARTICLE PUBLISHED IN PSYCHOLOGY TODAY, JANUARY 1975, "PLAY IS SERIOUS BUSINESS," DISCUSSES THE YERKES-DODSON LAW, A WELL-KNOWN RULE IN THE PSYCHOLOGY OF LEARNING. THIS LAW STATES THAT THE MORE COMPLEX A SKILL IS, THE LOWER THE OPTIMUM LEVEL OF MOTIVATION REQUIRED TO LEARN IT. TOO MUCH MOTIVATIONAL AROUSAL CAN INTERFERE WITH LEARNING. BRUNER NOTES THAT BY DEEMPHASIZING THE IMPORTANCE OF THE GOAL, PLAY MAY SERVE TO REDUCE EXCESSIVE DRIVE AND THUS ENABLE PEOPLE TO LEARN MORE EASILY.

TO BETTER UNDERSTAND THIS, THINK OF TRYING TO LEARN TO BALANCE WHILE WALKING ACROSS A 2X4 THAT IS TEN FEET LONG AND ONLY 13" ABOVE THE GROUND. THIS WOULD NOT BE SUCH A DIFFICULT TASK TO MASTER. BUT WHAT IF YOU HAD TO LEARN WITH THE SAME BOARD TWELVE OR TWENTY FEET ABOVE THE GROUND? THE HEIGHTENED MOTIVATIONAL AROUSAL CAN WORK AGAINST THE RELAXED ATTITUDE NEEDED TO MASTER THIS TASK.

IN YET ANOTHER WAY PLAY CAN AID THE LEARNING PROCESS. WHEN ROTE LEARNING BECOMES DULL AND MONO-TONOUS, MAKING A GAME OUT OF LEARNING CAN GIVE THE NEEDED MOTIVATION TO CONTINUE USING REPETITION TO REINFORCE LEARNING. GIFTED STUDENTS ARE ESPECIALLY TURNED OFF BY DRILL, ROUTINE AND REPETITION. AS A RULE, GIFTED STUDENTS WILL PICK UP BASIC SKILLS VERY QUICKLY AND WON'T NEED THE REPETITION THAT MANY OTHER STUDENTS WILL NEED. BUT IF THERE IS A REASON TO INVOLVE THEM IN ROTE LEARNING, BY ADDING THE DIMENSION OF PLAY AND/OR HUMOR YOU HAVE ADDED A MORE COMPLEX, RICHER DIMENSION TO THE THOUGHT PROCESS WHICH WILL MORE LIKELY KEEP THEIR INTEREST BECAUSE IT IS MORE APT TO CHALLENGE AND INTRIGUE THEM.

THIS BOOK IS DESIGNED TO GUIDE YOU THROUGH THIS PROCESS WHICH WILL

expand... BRAIN POWER

THROUGH ACTIVITIES THAT FOSTER THE EXPERIENCING AND ENJOYMENT OF LEARNING.

CREATIVITY

What is it and how does it work?

FIRST OF ALL, CREATIVITY IS NOT A THING, IT IS A PROCESS. IT IS A <u>WAY</u> <u>OF</u> <u>THINKING</u> <u>AND</u> <u>OF</u> <u>DOING</u>. ANYTHING YOU DO CAN BE DONE CREATIVELY, BUT WHAT DOES THAT MEAN?

THINK OF CREATIVITY AS A WAY OF MAKING <u>NEW</u> CONNECTIONS OR <u>NEW</u> <u>LINKS</u>. IT IS THE

PROCESS (of linking

PREVIOUSLY UNRELATED PEOPLE, IDEAS, PROCESSESS AND/OR THINGS.

FOR EXAMPLE, A MAN WENT FOR A WALK ACROSS A FIELD ONLY TO END UP PULLING STICKER BURRS OFF HIS PANTS AND SOCKS. YEARS LATER HE SAW A NEW AND USEFUL WAY TO APPLY WHAT HE HAD EARLIER OBSERVED. THAT'S CREATIVITY, OR THINKING CREATIVELY.

Observation

LINKED TO

Problem

Observation

1. BURRS ARE A NUCLEUS OF HOOKS

2. MY SOCKS ARE A SURFACE OF LOOPS

3. WHEREVER THE BURR TOUCHES THE SOCK IT STICKS TIGHTLY

Aha! Velcro

Problem

1. A SYSTEM IS NEEDED TO MAKE A FLEXIBLE FASTENER THAT CAN ATTACH SECURELY AT ANY POINT.

2. AHA! VELCRO, A TAPE OF MILLIONS OF TINY HOOKS THAT WILL STICK TIGHTLY TO A SURFACE OF MILLIONS OF TINY LOOPS.

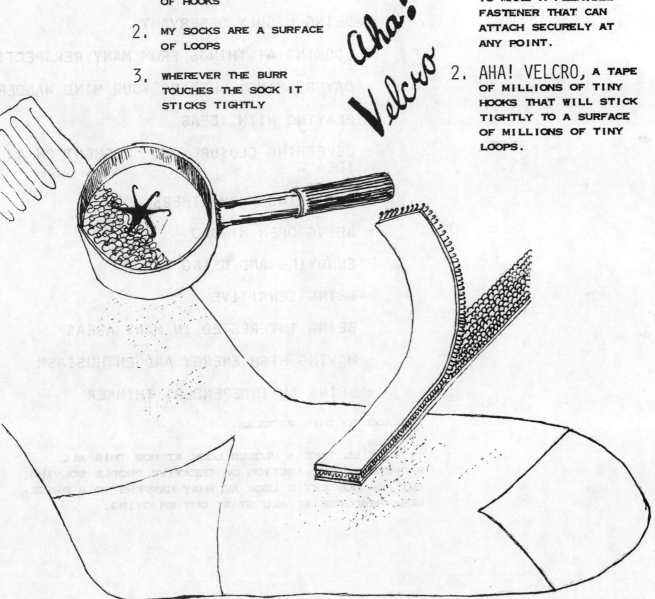

OFTEN A PROBLEM IS THE CATALYST TO THE CREATIVE PROCESS. BUT

- BEING HIGHLY CURIOUS

- BEING HIGHLY OBSERVANT

- LOOKING AT THINGS FROM MANY PERSPECTIV

- DAYDREAMING, LETTING YOUR MIND WANDER

- PLAYING WITH IDEAS

- DEFERRING CLOSURE AND JUDGMENT ON AN IDEA

- DIFFERING FROM OTHERS

- BEING OPEN MINDED

- ENJOYING AND USING HUMOR

- BEING SENSITIVE

- BEING INTERESTED IN MANY AREAS

- HAVING HIGH ENERGY AND ENTHUSIASM

- BEING AN INDEPENDENT THINKER

ALL ADD TO THIS PROCESS.

WE'LL TAKE A CLOSER LOOK AT HOW THIS ALL HAPPENS IN THE SECTION ON CREATIVE PROBLE SOLVING, BUT FOR NOW LET'S LOOK AT WHAT HAPPENS TO A PRICE-LESS RESOURCE WE ALL START OUT ENJOYING.

IN THE CHILDHOOD GAME OF "HEY, LET'S PLAY LIKE THIS BOX IS

A FORT OR -

A TURTLE SHELL OR -

A GIANT BROWNIE OR -

A RAIN CLOUD OR -

A SUITCASE OR -

A STABLE OR -

A LAKE . . ."

A CHILD'S CREATIVE IMAGINATION IS LINKING

THE CARDBOARD BOX

TO EARLIER IDEAS OR OBJECTS FROM THE CHILD'S EXPERIENCES.

WHEN THE LINK IS NEW TO THAT PERSON, THEN IT IS CREATIVE...OR CREATING A NEW RELATIONSHIP BETWEEN TWO PREVIOUSLY UNRELATED OBJECTS.

IF ANOTHER CHILD PICKS UP THIS SAME IDEA AND COPIES IT, THE SECOND CHILD IS NOT THINKING CREATIVELY.

BUT SUPPOSE A THIRD CHILD PICKS UP THE IDEA OF THE FIRST CHILD AND ADDS A NEW LINK TO IT. FOR EXAMPLE: "LET'S PRETEND THIS BOX IS A GIANT BROWNIE WITH RAISINS IN IT AND OUR TENNIS SHOES CAN BE THE GIANT RAISINS."

THE THIRD CHILD IS THINKING CREATIVELY BY CONNECT- ING, OR LINKING A NEW IDEA.

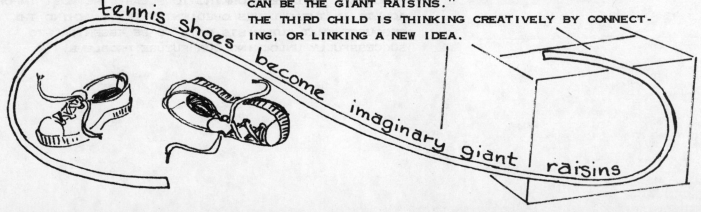

tennis shoes become imaginary giant raisins

LET'S SEE WHAT HAPPENS TO THIS VALUABLE CREATIVE RESOURCE IN CHILDREN. DUDLEY LYNCH, A LEADING WRITER ON CREATIVITY, NOTES IN A RECENT ARTICLE IN DALLAS/DECEMBER 78

At Buffalo's Creative Education Foundation, Dr. Ruth B. Noller and Angelo Biondo, editor of the JOURNAL OF CREATIVE BEHAVIOR, report that we are all strongly right-brained--and highly creative--as very young children. One study indicated that 90 percent of all children are highly creative until age five. Then within two years, the seeds of an immense tragedy appear: the number of highly creative children drops to 10 percent. In another year, only two percent of the population is left to meet the needs for extreme creativity for the other 98.

BUT WHY THE EXTREME LOSS OF CREATIVITY? WE NOTE THAT THE GREATEST DROP COINCIDES WITH BEGINNING SCHOOL. DOES THIS GREAT LOSS HAVE TO HAPPEN? IS THERE ANOTHER OPTION? AND ONCE LOST, CAN ANY OF THE CREATIVITY BE REGAINED OR REACTIVATED?

HOME AND SCHOOL ARE GENERALLY WORKING HARD (DURING THE AGES OF SIX, SEVEN AND EIGHT) TO TEACH A CHILD TO CONFORM TO THE RULES OF SOCIETY. THE A, B, C's, COUNTING, RULES OF BEHAVIOR...SO MUCH OF WHAT A CHILD IS LEARNING IS THROUGH ROTE MEMORY OR CONFORMING BEHAVIOR. THE MESSAGE IS LOUD AND CLEAR, "DO IT THE WAY YOU ARE TOLD." THERE IS LITTLE TIME OR ENCOURAGE-MENT FOR ORIGINAL IDEAS, AND NON-CONFORMING BEHAVIOR IS GENERALLY NOT ENCOURAGED AND OFTEN PUNISHED.

AND YET THESE ARE THE INGREDIENTS OF THE CREATIVE PROCESS. CHILDREN WORKING TO PLEASE THE MOST IMPORTANT ADULTS IN THEIR LIVES OBEDIENTLY LEAVE BEHIND THE RESOURCE THAT FUTURISTS NOTE TO BE ESSENTIAL TO SUCCESSFULLY UNLOCKING OUR FUTURE PROBLEMS.

BUT WHAT IF THERE WERE A BALANCE BETWEEN TIME FOR CHILDREN TO LEARN THOSE IMPORTANT CONFORMING SKILLS (FOR BASIC SKILLS AND SAFETY RULES ARE ALL VITAL AND NECESSARY) AND TIME TO BE ORIGINAL, TO USE ONE'S OWN IDEAS, AND BOTH WERE APPRECIATED EQUALLY? THE WORK OF DR. PAUL TORRANCE, DR. J. PAUL GUILFORD AND MANY OTHERS INDICATES THAT WHEN YOUNGSTERS ARE GIVEN REPEATED OPPORTUNITIES TO USE CREATIVE THINKING AND CREATIVE PROBLEM-SOLVING, THEY DO INCREASE IN THEIR ABILITY IN THESE AND OTHER RELATED AREAS. IN PROGRAMS WHERE THERE IS A BALANCE BETWEEN CONFORMING AND CREATIVE LEARNING, BOTH PROCESSES DEVELOP AND SUPPORT THE REST OF THE LEARNING PROCESS.

THIS COLLECTION OF LEARNING EXPERIENCES IS DESIGNED TO STIMULATE AND ENCOURAGE THE DEVELOPMENT OF CREATIVITY AND CREATIVE PROBLEM-SOLVING SKILLS.

Daydreaming & Imagery as Processes to Expand Brain Power

IN A CONFERENCE ON EDUCATION AND THE FUTURE HELD IN THE LATE 1960's, A TEAM INCLUDING REPRESENTATIVES FROM THE NATIONAL AERONAUTICS AND SPACE ADMINISTRATION POINTED OUT THAT MOST OF THE CURRICULUM THEN BEING TAUGHT IN ELEMENTARY SCHOOLS WOULD BECOME OBSOLETE BY THE TIME THE CHILDREN IT SERVED WERE ADULTS. INFORMATION AND TECHNOLOGY ARE COMPOUNDING AND CHANGING SO RAPIDLY THAT THEY CALL FOR A REASSESSMENT OF THE CURRENT CURRICULUM AND TEACHING PROCESSESS. WHEN PRESSED TO TAKE THE PROBLEM FARTHER AND TELL US WHAT WE SHOULD BE TEACHING IN SCHOOLS, THE CONCLUSION WAS THAT IMAGINATION, CREATIVE PROBLEM SOLVING AND THE MENTAL HEALTH TO PUT THESE TO CONSTRUCTIVE USE WILL NEVER GROW OBSOLETE AND WILL ALWAYS BE VITAL TO A SURVIVING AND THRIVING SOCIETY. (IT WAS NOTED THAT UNLESS A PERSON HAS THE SELF-CONFIDENCE AND POSITIVE SELF-IMAGE NECESSARY TO PUT HIS/HER GOOD IDEAS INTO PRACTICE, THESE IDEAS CAN END UP BENEFITING NO ONE.)

AS AN ELEMENTARY TEACHER I WAS ALSO STUNNED TO HEAR THAT MEMBERS OF THE SPACE TEAM WERE BEING TRAINED TO DAYDREAM FROM 20 MINUTES (BUILDING THEIR TOLERANCE SLOWLY) TO TWO HOURS EACH DAY BECAUSE IT IS IN THIS STATE THAT HIGHLY CREATIVE SOLUTIONS EMERGE. I HAD JUST SENT A THIRD GRADER HOME WITH A NOTE TO HIS PARENTS SAYING, "MARK IS SUCH A BRIGHT BOY. HE COULD DO SO WELL IF HE WOULD JUST LEARN TO STOP WASTING TIME BY DAYDREAMING." IT WAS WITH SOME EMBARRASSMENT THAT I INVITED MARK AND HIS PARENTS TO MEET ME AFTER SCHOOL THE NEXT WEEK TO SHARE WITH THEM WHAT I HAD LEARNED ABOUT THE VALUE OF DAYDREAMING. DR. MARY MEEKER NOTED THAT IN RESEARCH MEASURING BRAIN ACTIVITY, MORE OF THE BRAIN IS ACTIVE WHEN A PERSON IS DAYDREAMING THAN WHEN "ON TASK".

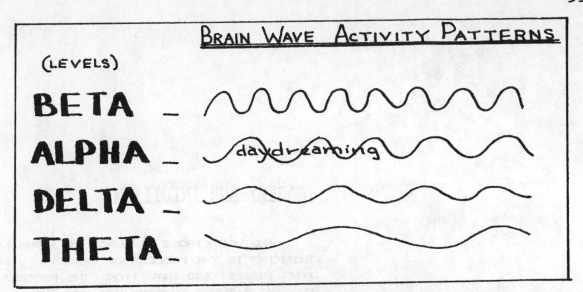

BRAIN WAVE ACTIVITY PATTERNS

(LEVELS)

BETA _

ALPHA _ daydreaming

DELTA _

THETA _

IN STUDYING LEVELS OF BRAIN WAVES WE LEARN THAT WHEN THE BRAIN IS CONCENTRATING OR "ON TASK", THIS LEVEL IS CALLED BETA. IN THIS LEVEL THE WAVES ARE MORE ACTIVE AND FREQUENT, MUCH LIKE A MUSCLE IS TENSE AND TIGHTER WHEN ACTIVE AND WORKING.

THE NEXT LEVEL IS CALLED ALPHA. THIS IS THE DAYDREAM STATE, AND WHEN IN ALPHA THE BRAIN WAVES ARE MORE RELAXED, LESS FREQUENT. IT IS IN THIS LEVEL THAT DR. ROLLO MAY IN HIS BOOK, THE COURAGE TO CREATE, NOTES THAT CREATIVE BREAKTHROUGHS OR THE "EUREKA!" EXPERIENCE HAPPENS. HE EXPLAINS THAT THE CENSOR OR THE FOCUSED BRAIN MUST BE OFF DUTY FOR THE CREATIVE LINKING TO HAPPEN. OUR SEEMINGLY CRAZY IDEAS ARE ABLE TO EMERGE AND MAKE THE CONNECTIONS NECESSARY FOR THE CREATIVE PROCESS TO HAPPEN.

THE THIRD AND FOURTH LEVELS ARE DELTA AND THETA. BOTH HAPPEN WHILE IN A SLEEP STATE. AND IN EACH OF THESE LEVELS THE BRAIN WAVES ARE SUCCESS- IVELY MORE RELAXED AND LESS FREQUENT.

THE IMPORTANT INSIGHT THAT EDUCATORS CAN GLEAN FROM ALL THIS IS THAT TYPICALLY TRADITIONAL EDUCATION PUTS A HIGH EMPHASIS ON THE BETA LEVEL (FOCUSED THINKING) AND DISCOUNTS OR OFTEN EVEN PUNISHES ALPHA LEVEL THINKING. BY LEARNING THAT ALPHA IS THE LEVEL WHERE CREATIVE BREAKTHROUGHS OCCUR, EDUCATORS MIGHT BE URGED TO INCREASE THE CURRICULUM EMPHASIS ON ALPHA LEVEL THINKING. A MORE REASONABLE BALANCE BETWEEN ALPHA AND BETA LEARNING COULD PROVIDE A RICH HARVEST OF GROWTH. REMEMBER THAT CREATIVITY IS FED BY BETA LEARNING EVEN THOUGH THE BREAKTHROUGH HAPPENS MOST OFTEN IN ALPHA. IT IS NOT A QUESTION OF WHICH IS BEST OR WHICH IS MOST IMPORTANT. BOTH ARE NECESSARY AND VALUABLE ASPECTS OF THINKING AND LEARNING, BUT THE BRAIN CAN BE STRONGER AND MORE PRODUCTIVE IF IT DRAWS ON AND INTEGRATES BOTH SOURCES.

IMAGERY AND INTUITION

ANOTHER STRONG RESOURCE OF ALPHA LEVEL
THINKING IS THE PROCESS OF IMAGERY (VISUALI-
ZING IMAGES) AND INTUITION (THE PROCESS OF
KNOWING WITHOUT KNOWING HOW YOU KNOW). MANY
BREAKTHROUGHS IN SCIENCE AND TECHNOLOGY HAVE
FIRST COME IN THE FORM OF AN IMAGE. THE DIS-
COVERY OF THE DNA MOLECULE AND THE BENZINE
RING FIRST OCCURRED AS AN IMAGE.

IT IS THOUGHT THAT CHILDREN ARE GENERALLY
VERY HIGHLY INTUITIVE BUT SLOWLY LOSE THIS
ABILITY. IT IS NO WONDER WHEN WE THINK OF HOW
TRADITIONAL EDUCATION REACTS TO A STUDENT WHO
KNOWS THE ANSWER BUT CANNOT TELL HOW S/HE KNOWS.
THE ACCUSATION OF CHEATING OR GETTING HELP FROM
ANOTHER IS OFTEN MADE. SO STUDENTS LEARN EARLY
THAT IT IS VERY RISKY TO OFFER INTUITIVE IDEAS.
WHAT IF, INSTEAD, EDUCATORS HELPED CHILDREN
LEARN TO RECOGNIZE AND HARVEST THEIR STRONG
INTUITIVE RESOURCE? AS TEACHERS WE CALL UPON
OUR INTUITION HEAVILY FOR SUCH DECISIONS AS
GRADING, SEATING ARRANGEMENTS, GROUPING, RESPOND-
ING TO PARENTS. WHY THEN DO WE DISCOUNT THIS
RESOURCE WITH OUR STUDENTS? I WOULD SUGGEST THAT
WE WERE NEVER HELPED TO UNDERSTAND AND APPRECIATE
OUR OWN INTUITION. AS WE DO, WE CAN REGAIN AND
SHARE THIS RICH RESOURCE WITH OUR STUDENTS.

WOOLGATHERING

HIGHLY CREATIVE PEOPLE SEEM TO SHARE THE CHARACTERISTIC OF FREQUENT WOOLGATHERING OR OF BEING HIGHLY CURIOUS AND ACTIVELY OBSERVANT. THEY COLLECT NEW IDEAS NOT BECAUSE THEY HAVE A NEED FOR THEM NOW BUT THEY KNOW THAT SOMEDAY THESE IDEAS MAY JUST "COME IN HANDY." AS THEY TAKE TIME TO LEARN IN DEPTH ABOUT ALL SORTS OF THINGS, THEY ARE BUILDING A RICH STOREHOUSE OF OBSERVATIONS AND UNDERSTANDINGS WHICH CAN LATER BE LINKED TO EMERGING PROBLEMS IN CREATIVE NEW SOLUTIONS.

ANOTHER FORM OF WOOLGATHERING THAT YOU MAY RECOGNIZE IN YOURSELF IS THE HABIT OF COLLECTING ALL SORTS OF CLUTTER - - - YARN, STRING, SCRAPS OF WRAPPING PAPER, EGG CARTONS, WIRE - - - NOT BECAUSE YOU HAVE AN IMMEDIATE NEED FOR THEM BUT BECAUSE YOU MIGHT NEED THEM SOME DAY.

HIGHLY CREATIVE PEOPLE TYPICALLY KNOW A GREAT DEAL ABOUT SEVERAL DIVERSE FIELDS OF STUDY. FOR EXAMPLE, THE MAN WHO INVENTED THE ARTIFICIAL HEART VALVE WAS FIRST A MUSICIAN (AND LEARNED A GREAT DEAL ABOUT THE INTERACTION OF RHYTHMS WHICH HE LATER TRANSFERRED TO UNDERSTANDING VARIOUS BODY RHYTHMS.) THEN HE BECAME AN ENGINEER IN FLUID DYNAMICS AND LATER A MEDICAL DOCTOR AND SURGEON. YOU CAN SEE THE GREAT ADVANTAGE HE HAD THROUGH HIS EXTENDED KNOWLEDGE IN THESE THREE VARIED FIELDS. EACH PART OF HIS LIFE SERVED AS A RICH WOOLGATHERING EXPERIENCE TO CONTRIBUTE TO HIS CREATIVE SOLUTION OF AN ARTIFICIAL HEART VALVE.

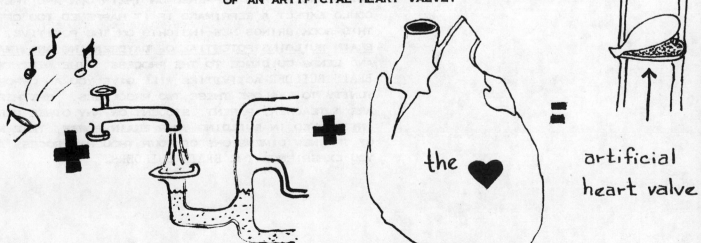

the ♥ = artificial heart valve

AS A FINAL NOTE ABOUT THE DAYDREAM STATE, SHEILA OSTRANDER AND LYNN SCHROEDER WITH NANCY OSTRANDER IN THEIR BOOK, SUPERLEARNING, REPORT ON AN AMAZING NEW FORM OF LEARNING PIONEERED IN BULGARIA. "BY TEACHING LANGUAGE WHILE STUDENTS ARE IN ALPHA, LISTENING TO MUSIC AND RELAXED BUT NOT FOCUSED ON THE CONTENT, STUDENTS CAN DEVELOP SUPERMEMORY AND LEARN TWO TO TEN TIMES FASTER." THIS PROCESS, CALLED SUGGESTOLOGY, "IS A LEARNING SYSTEM THAT LETS ADULTS LEARN A LANGUAGE IN FOUR WEEKS AND SCHOOL CHILDREN COVER A GRADE IN A FEW MONTHS." SUPERLEARNING IS A COMPLEX SYSTEM AND TO LEARN ABOUT IT IN DEPTH YOU ARE ENCOURAGED TO REFER TO THE BOOK. BUT THE GENERAL CONCEPT IS CAUSING EDUCATORS TO TAKE A FRESH LOOK AT WHAT IS STRESSED IN SCHOOLS AND HOW MATERIAL IS PRESENTED.

THESE SEVERAL NEW LEARNING CONCEPTS DO SUPPORT A CREDIBLE RATIONALE FOR BUILDING MORE TIME INTO THE GENERAL CURRICULUM AT ALL LEVELS TO ENABLE STUDENTS TO LEARN THE PROCESS AND ROLE OF DAYDREAMING AND IMAGERY FOR IDEA GENERATION AND CREATIVE PROBLEM-SOLVING. IT IS JUST AS IMPORTANT THAT STUDENTS LEARN THE WHY AS THE HOW BECAUSE TRADITIONALLY MOST STUDENTS BELIEVED THAT, WHILE SERVING AS A PLEASANT DIVERSION, DAYDREAMING WAS NOT PRODUCTIVE. STUDENTS HAVE BEEN DAYDREAMING AND IMAGING FOR AS LONG AS THERE HAVE BEEN STUDENTS. BUT USUALLY THIS HAPPENED ON THEIR OWN AND THEY COULD EXPECT A REPRIMAND IF IT HAPPENED TOO OFTEN. THIS BOOK BRINGS NEW INSIGHTS ON THE POSITIVE, BRAIN BUILDING POTENTIAL OF DAYDREAMING AND IMAGERY AND LENDS GUIDANCE TO THE PROCESS. THE NEXT TWO BRAIN BUILDER ACTIVITIES WILL GIVE YOU AN OPPOR- TUNITY TO EXPLORE THESE TWO PROCESSES. WHETHER YOU ARE A TEACHER, PARENT, STUDENT OR ANY OTHER PERSON INTERESTED IN BUILDING YOUR BRAIN POWER, TAKE NOTE OF THE NEW DIMENSIONS OF YOUR THOUGHT PROCESS AS YOU EXPERIENCE THE BRAIN BUILDERS.

What if There Was a Dandruff Machine Behind Your Left Ear?

What would it look like? How would it work? Would funny little invisible creatures operate the machine? Would the machine be invisible? Imagine that you can pull your nose gently to cause your eyes to be able to see this absurd contraption. What will it be like? What if it had a color dial so you could dial blue, pink or lavender dandruff? What if the dandruff sprouted legs or wings? What if the "ON" button got stuck and you began to be buried in dandruff? What other ways can you think of to create a surprise? Let your mind wander and imagine other parts of this fantasy.

To SUPER SNOW WHITE DANDRUFF MAKER

science/Technology

Children are engineers! From the time they first pull a toy toward themselves on a blanket we see this ability developing. The process of identifying a need and finding a way to make it happen. . .that's what it's all about.

Children arrive with a lively curiosity; how does a clock work?

What makes a frog hop?

How high is high?

Why is rain wet?

The world or nature and science can speak vividly to these interests.

what if...

you could design and build a machine to solve any problem? For example, design a machine to pick up your clothes and straighten your room or one to take out the garbage for you. Or you might invent a system to resolve arguments.

How would your machine work? Would it make sounds, have an alarm, have buttons, flashing lights, a certain smell, produce smoke? Show with paint, colored markers or scrap materials how your machine would look and work!

concepts

that might be developed:

creating new industrial designs, communicating directions, understanding cause and effect relationships, inventing systems, and evaluating structure.

A Committee of Witches Are in the Market For a New Vehicle

They are writing to Detroit to ask that something new be designed for them for their annual Halloween flights through space. "We'd like something less drafty. It's no wonder that a witches' hair is always blown about and stringy. How would your hair look if you had to fly about on a drafty old broom?"

Imagine you are one of the witches helping this committee brainstorm possible specifications for the new vehicle. Would you wish for a CB to communicate with other witches and with truckers? Would you want a two-seater so that your cat would have a secure place to sit or perhaps a four-seater so that you could take friends with you? Would you request windshield wipers, a moon roof, cruise control, radar to warn of other aircraft in the area or possible stars in your path? Surely a witch would never be seen piloting an ordinary space craft.

Now imagine that you are a vehicle designer who receives this unusual request. What kind of strange and wonderful flying machine can you invent? Which mobile will be the next witchmobile?

art

This card suggests a fresh approach to traditional holidays. To ask a student to reproduce look-alike pumpkins or to color in outlines of stereotyped witches or other traditional images conveys to a student a "don't think for yourself" message. This message inhibits and limits creative thinking. Instead, students might be invited to invent, imagine and apply problem-solving to open-ended questions arising from a holiday idea.

Perhaps pumpkins are in revolt! "Why must we ALWAYS be the vegetable that gets carved out for Halloween jack-o-lanterns? Why not give us a break this year and find another vegetable or fruit to use for your jack-o-lantern sculpture? Why not use a water-melon, a banana or an apple? Maybe a candle could be perched on top of a face carved in an apple. Or perhaps spices and candy could be added with toothpicks such as marshmallow eyes and clove teeth stuck to a bana-o-lantern."

Excellent mood music to stimulate these activities: Dance Macabre by Charles Camille Saint-Säens

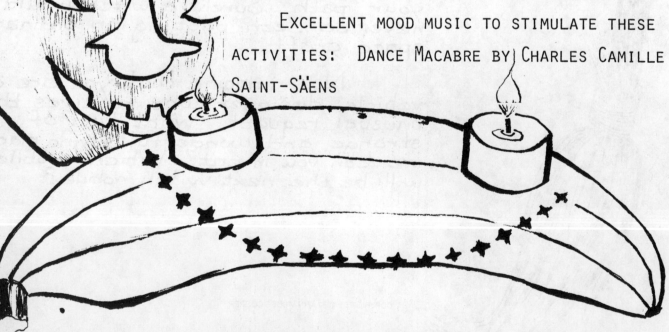

BRAINSTORMING

A BASIC PROCESS TO INCREASE YOUR CREATIVE
FLOW OF IDEAS COMES FROM ALEX OSBORN'S IDEAS IN
<u>APPLIED IMAGINATION</u>. THIS PROCESS IS CALLED
BRAINSTORMING. THE RULES ARE SIMPLE.

1. <u>TURN OFF THE EDITOR OR CENSOR IN YOUR BRAIN.</u>

MOST OF US AUTOMATICALLY CHECK OUT EACH
IDEA THAT OCCURS TO US BEFORE WE SAY IT OUT LOUD
OR WRITE IT DOWN. THIS IS BECAUSE WE DON'T WANT
TO "LOOK FOOLISH" OR "MAKE A MISTAKE" OR "SOUND
DUMB." DID YOU EVER STOP TO THINK ABOUT HOW
FOOLISH AND OUTRAGEOUS ALMOST ALL NEW IDEAS SOUNDED
BEFORE PEOPLE GOT USED TO THEM AND LEARNED TO TAKE
THEM FOR GRANTED?

FOR EXAMPLE, IF YOU LIVED IN SPAIN IN 1491 AND YOU HAD STUDIED GEOGRAPHY IN THE FINEST UNIVERSITIES WITH THE VERY BEST SCHOLARS, YOU KNEW THAT THE WORLD WAS FLAT. WHAT WOULD YOU THINK ABOUT A STRANGE GUY NAMED COLUMBUS WHO WENT AROUND TRYING TO GET MONEY TO BUY SHIPS AND A CREW SO THAT HE COULD SAIL AROUND THE WORLD? YOUR GOOD EDUCATION WOULD TELL YOU THIS GUY WAS CRAZY!

OR, WHAT IF YOU LIVED IN THE YEARS BEFORE AIR TRAVEL? ALL YOU HAD EVER SEEN FLY IN THE SKY WERE BIRDS, CLOUDS AND, PERHAPS, KITES.

NOW YOU LIVE IN THE LITTLE TOWN OF KITTY HAWK, NORTH CAROLINA, AND HEAR JOKES ABOUT TWO CRAZY BROTHERS, WILBUR AND ORVILLE WRIGHT, WHO ARE TRYING TO GET A WILD CONTRAPTION THAT WEIGHS OVER 2,000 POUNDS OFF THE GROUND <u>WITH THEM IN IT</u>! BOY, WOULD THAT MAKE EVERYONE SLAP HIS THIGHS WITH LAUGHTER!

AND WOULD YOU HAVE WANTED TO OWN A TELEPHONE OR A TELEVISION SET IN SALEM, CONNECTICUT, BACK IN EARLY COLONIAL TIMES WHEN THEY WERE BURNING PEOPLE FOR BEING WITCHES IF THEY SEEMED TO BE A LITTLE UNUSUAL OR HAD WHAT SEEMED TO BE SUPER-NATURAL POWERS? CAN YOU IMAGINE WHAT THEY WOULD HAVE THOUGHT ABOUT YOU IF YOU SAID, "WAIT A MINUTE AND LET'S SEE WHAT THE CHANNEL 4 NEWS HAS TO SAY ABOUT THE WEEK-END WEATHER." OR, "LET'S PLACE A CALL TO THE QUEEN OF ENGLAND TO DISCUSS OUR DIS-AGREEMENTS OVER TAXATION?"

THE POINT IS THAT ANY NEW IDEA SOUNDS STRANGE AT FIRST AND IF THIS STRANGENESS SCARES YOU OFF, YOU WON'T EVER TELL ANYONE ABOUT YOUR BEST IDEAS.

2. THE SECOND RULE OF BRAINSTORMING IS TO <u>SAY EACH IDEA OUT LOUD</u> AS IT OCCURS TO YOU. SOMETIMES THE VALUE OF AN IDEA IS THAT IT TRIGGERS OR STIMULATES ANOTHER IDEA.

3. THIS IS CALLED <u>HITCHHIKING</u> OR <u>PIGGYBACKING IDEAS</u>.

4. <u>SUSPEND JUDGMENT</u>. AVOID COMMENTS SUCH AS, "GOOD IDEA", OR "THAT IDEA STINKS". EITHER WAY CAN GET YOU AND YOUR TEAM OFF TRACK AND INTO JUDGING WHEN THE FIRST AND PRIMARY CONCERN SHOULD BE FOR A

5. <u>FREE, UN-INTERRUPTED FLOW OF IDEAS</u>!

6. <u>EXPECT TO BE OUTRAGEOUS</u>. HUMOR AND OFF-
    THE-WALL COMMENTS ARE ALL PART OF RELEASING
    YOUR CREATIVE IMAGINATION. OFTEN THERE IS A
    KERNEL OF TRUTH WITHIN A HUMOROUS REMARK, SO
    LET ALL KINDS OF IDEAS FLOW.

7. <u>RECORD ALL IDEAS</u>. A TAPE RECORDER CAN DO
    THIS PART EASILY AND EFFICIENTLY. OR EACH
    PERSON CAN WRITE DOWN HIS/HER OWN IDEAS AFTER
    SAYING THEM OUT LOUD FOR THE GROUP TO HEAR.

8. <u>CONTROL THE GROUP SIZE</u>. GROUPS OF FOUR
    OR SIX WORK WELL. THEN EVERYONE CAN BE
    HEARD AND THERE ARE ENOUGH PEOPLE TO STIMULATE
    EACH OTHER'S THINKING BUT NOT SO MANY TO MAKE
    MANAGEMENT A PROBLEM. EXPERIENCED TEACHERS
    REPORT THAT ANY SYSTEM THAT ARBITRARILY MIXES
    UP STUDENTS (COUNT OFF BY 5'S OR, EVERYONE
    WHOSE NAME BEGINS WITH A B GO TO THE TABLE)
    WILL INCREASE THE EFFECTIVENESS OF THE ACTIVITY.
    BEFORE YOU START, HAVE EACH GROUP SELECT A
    LEADER.

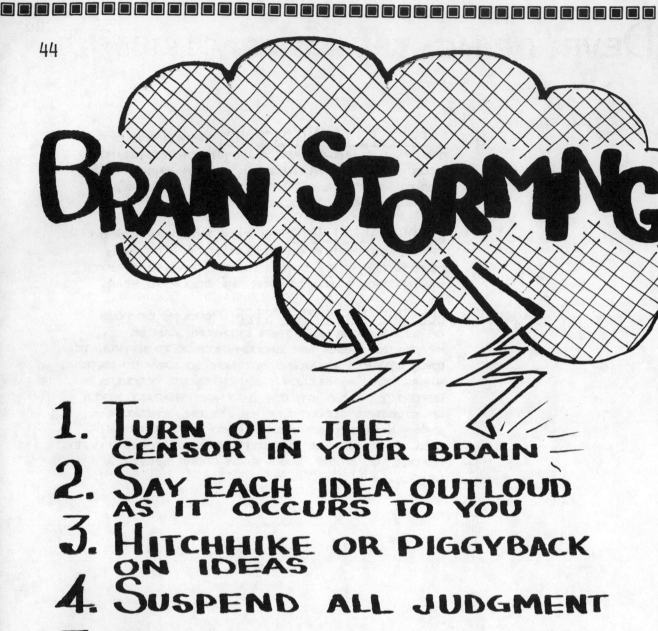

BRAIN STORMING

1. Turn off the censor in your brain
2. Say each idea outloud as it occurs to you
3. Hitchhike or piggyback on ideas
4. Suspend all judgment
5. Encourage a free, uninterrupted flow of ideas
6. Expect to be outrageous
7. Record all ideas
8. Control size of group

DEVELOPING THE CHARACTERISTICS
OF Creative
Thinking

DR. E. PAUL TORRANCE HAS SPENT THE LAST TWENTY-FIVE YEARS RESEARCHING CREATIVITY AND HOW ONE CAN NURTURE THIS IMPORTANT PROCESS. HE ALSO HAS DESIGNED THE NATIONAL FUTURE PROBLEM-SOLVING COMPETITION TO ENCOURAGE SYSTEMATIC APPLICATION AND DEVELOPMENT OF THESE SKILLS. TORRANCE, IN HIS RESEARCH, NOTED THE FOLLOWING FOUR CHARACTER-ISTICS OF CREATIVE THINKING. THESE CHARACTERISTICS ARE:

1 FLUENCY — THE NUMBER OF DIFFERENT RELE-VANT IDEAS

2 FLEXIBILITY — THE NUMBER OF SHIFTS IN THINKING OR DIFFERENT CATE-GORIES OF RESPONSE

3 ELABORATION — THE NUMBER OF DIFFERENT IDEAS USED IN WORKING OUT THE DETAILS OF AN IDEA

4 ORIGINALITY — THE NUMBER OF STATISTICALLY INFREQUENT RESPONSES THAT SHOW CREATIVE INTELLECTUAL ENERGY.

OTHERS IN THE FIELD OF CREATIVE THINKING HAVE ADDED A FIFTH CHARACTERISTIC:

5 EVALUATION — THE PROCESS OF SELECTING, TESTING AND REVISING ONE OR MORE IDEAS FROM A LARGER GROUP OF IDEAS THAT HAVE BEEN GENERATED.

THE FOLLOWING SECTION HAS ACTIVITIES TO DEVELOP THE USE OF EACH OF THESE FIVE CHARACTERISTICS.

5 CHARACTERISTICS of Creative Thinking

1 *fluency* — THE NUMBER OF DIFFERENT RELEVANT IDEAS.

2 FLEXIBILITY — THE NUMBER OF SHIFTS IN THINKING OR DIFFERENT CATEGORIES OF RESPONSE

3 *ELABORATION* — THE NUMBER OF DIFFERENT IDEAS USED IN WORKING OUT THE DETAILS OF AN IDEA.

4 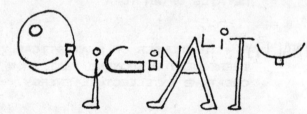 — THE NUMBER OF STATISTICALLY INFREQUENT RESPONSES THAT SHOW CREATIVE INTELLECTUAL ENERGY.

5 EVALUATION — THE PROCESS OF SELECTING, TESTING AND REVISING ONE OR MORE IDEAS FROM A LARGER GROUP OF IDEAS THAT HAVE BEEN GENERATED.

FROM THE RESEARCH OF E. PAUL TORRANCE

47

STIMULATING CREATIVE THINKING

1 WORKING FOR *fluency*

FLUENCY – THE NUMBER OF DIFFERENT RELEVANT IDEAS.

IF YOU WERE GOING TO CHOOSE A BEST FRIEND OR A NEW HOUSE, WOULD YOU RATHER HAVE TWO OR SIXTY-EIGHT POSSIBLE CHOICES? THE BEST CANDIDATE MIGHT BE ONE OF THE FIRST TWO. BUT STATISTICALLY YOUR CHANCES ARE BETTER IF YOU HAVE A LARGER NUMBER OF POSSIBLE CHOICES.

BEHIND THE RATIONALE FOR LEARNING TO GENERATE MORE IDEAS (OR TO INCREASE FLUENCY OF THINKING) IS THE RATIONALE THAT

QUANTITY of ideas can lead to QUALITY!

A GOOD ACTIVITY DESIGNED TO INCREASE FLUENCY OF THINKING IS CALLED,

"WHAT CAN IT BE?"

WHAT CAN IT BE ?

A BRAIN EXERCISE TO STIMULATE *fluency.*

1. START WITH A SIMPLE OBJECT SUCH AS A TOILET PAPER ROLL OR A PLAIN BOX OR A BLACKBOARD ERASER.

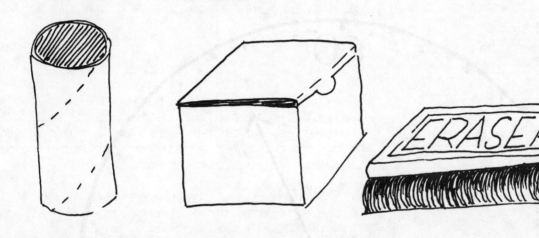

2. LIMIT GROUP SIZE TO FOUR OR SIX PEOPLE SO THERE WILL BE ENOUGH TO STIMULATE CROSS-GENERATION OF IDEAS AND FEW ENOUGH SO THAT EACH PERSON'S MIND IS ACTIVE.

3. PASS THE OBJECT AROUND SO THAT EACH PERSON CAN HANDLE IT AND EXAMINE IT FROM ALL ANGLES.

4. ASK EACH PERSON TO RECORD HIS/HER IDEAS (AND OBSERVE THE OTHER RULES OF BRAINSTORMING).

5. IN SIXTY SECONDS, HOW MANY DIFFERENT IDEAS CAN YOU GENERATE FOR WHAT YOUR OBJECT CAN BE?

AT THE END OF SIXTY SECONDS, ASK EACH GROUP TO MAKE A FLUENCY COUNT (THE TOTAL NUMBER OF DIFFERENT IDEAS GENERATED BY THE GROUP).

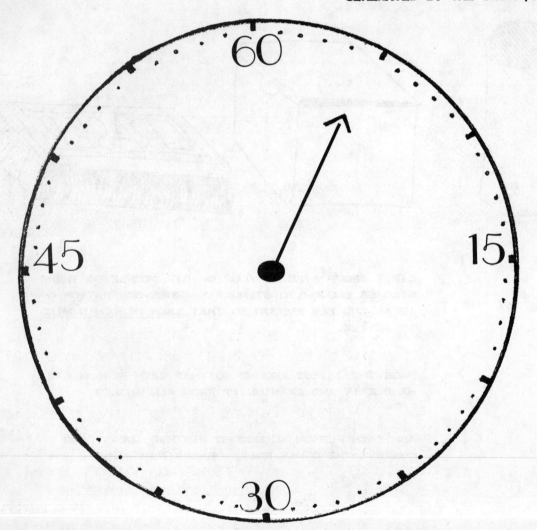

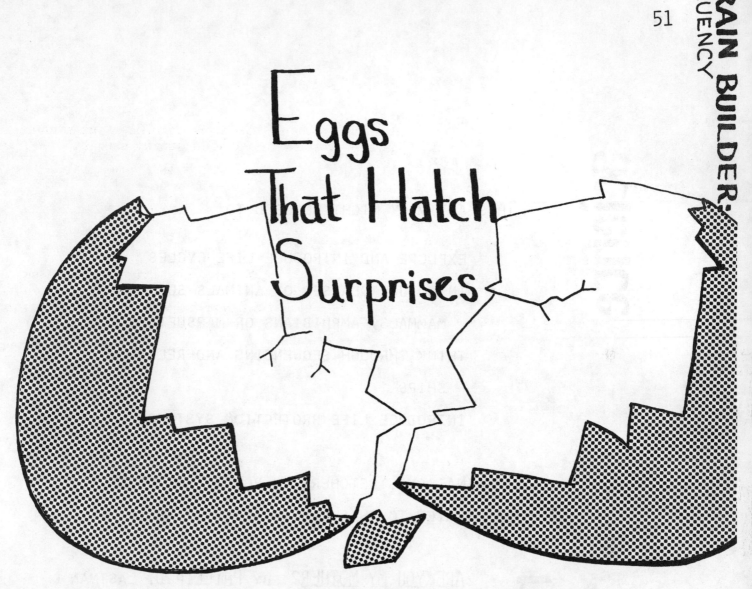

Eggs That Hatch Surprises

Did you know that turtles, lizards, and alligators are hatched from eggs? A turtle egg hatching might be a great surprise if it happened in the nest of a mother duck!

What other surprising creature might break out of an egg? Maybe it's magic or a bit of foolishness hatches out such as a baby mail box, a baby dump truck or an infant space lab. Experiment with some creative linking and imagine something unusual and unexpected being hatched from an egg.

science

THIS ACTIVITY MIGHT BE USED TO:

EXPLORE AND INTRODUCE LIFE CYCLES

INTRODUCE CLASSES OF ANIMALS SUCH AS

MAMMALS, AMPHIBIANS OR MARSUPIALS

THINK THROUGH SEQUENCING AND RELATION-

SHIPS

INTRODUCE LIFE PROTECTION SYSTEMS.

IMAGINATION STRETCHERS IN BOOKS THAT COULD

BE RELATED TO THIS VISUAL ACTIVITY ARE:

reading

ARE YOU MY MOTHER? BY PHILLIP D. EASTMAN

HORTON HATCHES A WHO? BY DR. SUESS

THE EGG BOOK BY JACK KENT

A falling leaf becomes...

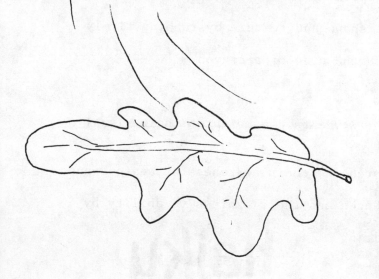

It's fall and the leaves are turning autumn colors and falling, one by one, to the ground. How many ways can you think of to use a falling leaf? Can it be a bug elevator (one-way only)? Could it be a parachute for a worm? Whose umbrella might it be? Or who might use it for air mail stationery? What else can you imagine?

science

creative writing

This activity might lead into a science unit identifying different types of trees by their leaf shapes.

Students might learn to make leaf rubbings by laying thin paper such as newsprint over a leaf and picking up the shape and texture by rubbing firmly with the side of a crayon.

Students can heighten their visual awareness, their awareness of seasons and changes and their expressive ability by writing **haiku**

Haiku is poetry that is written in three lines with a 5 - 7 - 5 syllable pattern.

tiny new leaves sprout
slowly carefully at first
then large outstretched hand

Georgia
age 7

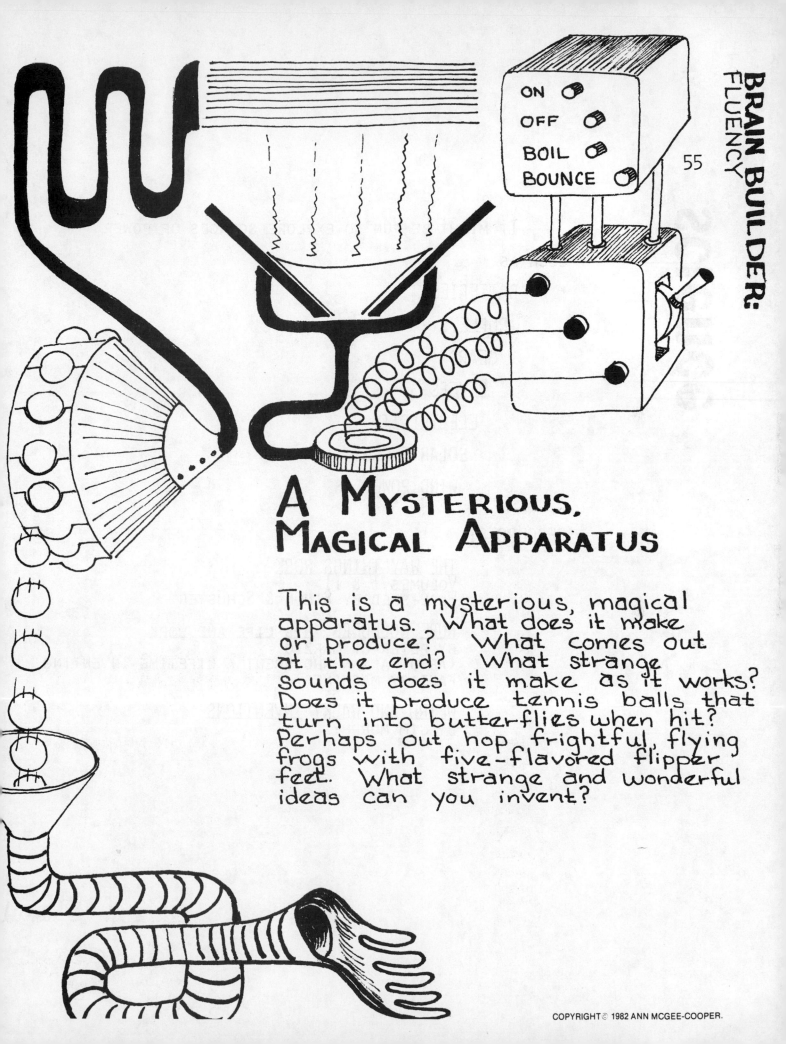

ON
OFF
BOIL
BOUNCE

55

A MYSTERIOUS, MAGICAL APPARATUS

This is a mysterious, magical apparatus. What does it make or produce? What comes out at the end? What strange sounds does it make as it works? Does it produce tennis balls that turn into butterflies when hit? Perhaps out hop frightful, flying frogs with five-flavored flipper feet. What strange and wonderful ideas can you invent?

science

IT MIGHT BE FUN TO EXPLORE SOURCES OF POWER

SUCH AS

BATTERIES

PULLEYS

GEARS

LEVERS

ELECTRICITY

SOLAR ENERGY

WIND POWER

RESOURCES:

THE WAY THINGS WORK
VOLUMES I & II
PUBLISHED BY SIMON & SCHUSTER

RUBE GOLDBERG, HIS LIFE AND WORK
BY PETER C. MARZIO
(ABOUT A MAN WHO SPENT A LIFETIME INVENTING
FANTASY MACHINES)

WEIRD AND WACKY INVENTIONS
BY JIM MURPHY

BUILDING *flexible* MORE *thinking*

flexibility. THE NUMBER OF SHIFTS IN THINKING OR DIFFERENT CATEGORIES OF RESPONSE.

PART II

CONTINUING THE ACTIVITY, "WHAT CAN IT BE?" YOU WILL NEED TO BE IN GROUPS OF FOUR TO SIX, AND EACH GROUP WILL NEED A SIMPLE OBJECT SUCH AS A BOX, PAPER ROLL OR CONE SHAPE AS AN IDEA STARTER. WARM UP FOR THIS ACTIVITY BY FIRST PLAYING, "WHAT CAN IT BE?" FOR FLUENCY. (SEE PAGE 49)

1. NOW, ASK EACH GROUP TO PUT THE OBJECT THEY ARE USING AS AN IDEA STARTER WHERE EACH PERSON CAN SEE IT.

2. LISTEN SILENTLY AS SUGGESTIONS TO STIMULATE FLEXIBLE THINKING ARE GIVEN BY A LEADER.

3. EACH PERSON SHOULD MAKE A MARK ON HIS/HER PAPER EACH TIME S/HE THINKS OF A NEW IDEA NOT GENERATED IN THE FLUENCY EXERCISE.

EX: ⊬⊬⊬ ⊬⊬⊬ ||

4. A LEADER THEN READS THE FOLLOWING IMAGI-NATION STIMULATORS OUT LOUD, SLOWLY AND WITH FREQUENT PAUSES TO ALLOW TIME TO GENERATE IDEAS.

"YOUR OBJECT HAS TO DO WITH SOUND. IT MAKES MUSIC OR IS PART OF AN ALARM SYSTEM...IT MAY MEASURE, MUFFLE OR GENERATE SOUNDS...IT IS PART OF A JAZZ BAND, A MUSIC BOX, A STORM ALERT SYSTEM, A CRICKET'S CHIRPING DEVICE. WHAT CAN IT BE? (ALLOW A FEW MOMENTS FOR PARTICI-PANTS TO THINK.)

YOUR OBJECT IS EDIBLE. IT IS CHOCO-
LATE, A FORM OF PROTEIN, MEAT OR FISH.
IT IS PASTA, A HOLIDAY TREAT, SOME
FORM OF BREAD, A KITCHEN TOOL. IT
STORES FOOD. IT IS DRINKABLE, IT'S
FROZEN, IT'S PUDDING. IT'S A VEGETABLE,
FRUIT OR ORGANIC FOOD. WHAT CAN IT BE?
(ALLOW TIME TO THINK.)

YOUR OBJECT IS 100 TIMES AS SMALL AS
YOU SEE IT NOW. WHAT CAN IT BE? IT
IS INSIDE YOUR BODY, PART OF YOUR EAR,
YOUR ESOPHAGUS, YOUR HEART, YOUR LIVER,
YOUR KIDNEYS, YOUR BRAIN. IT'S TRAV-
ELING IN YOUR BLOOD STREAM, IT'S A
FOREIGN SUBSTANCE, IT'S SOMETHING THAT
WILL MAKE YOU WELL. IT'S A THOUGHT IN
YOUR MIND...ABOUT WHAT? (ALLOW TIME TO
THINK.)

YOUR OBJECT IS 1000 TIMES LARGER THAN
YOU SEE IT NOW. IT IS PART OF THE
UNIVERSE. IT EXPLAINS EVOLUTION. IT
IS PART OF FUTURE SPACE SYSTEMS. IT'S
PART OF A SYSTEM OF ECOLOGY. IT IS
FANTASY FROM A FAIRY TALE OF GIANTS
AND GNOMES. WHAT CAN IT BE? (PAUSE.)

YOUR OBJECT IS MANY OF ITSELF ALL GROUPED
TOGETHER LIKE A HONEYCOMB OR RAINDROPS
IN A GIANT STORM CLOUD. WHAT CAN IT BE?
(PAUSE.)

YOUR OBJECT IS ONLY A PART OF SOMETHING,
A TOOL, A DENTAL INSTRUMENT, A TOY. IT
IS PART OF A VEHICLE...FOUND UNDER THE
HOOD...THE STEERING MECHANISM...THE
ENERGY SYSTEM...THE MAPPING SYSTEM...
THE HIGHWAY, RAILS, AIR, PATH THAT IT
FOLLOWS. WHAT CAN IT BE? (PAUSE.)

YOUR OBJECT HAS TO DO WITH WEAPONS, WAR, HATE, DESTRUCTION. WHAT CAN IT BE? (PAUSE.)

YOUR OBJECT IS PART OF A FEELING SUCH AS LOVE, FRIENDSHIP, CARING, REJECTION, LONELINESS. WHAT CAN IT BE? (PAUSE.)

YOUR OBJECT IS PART OF THE SYSTEM USED TO CREATE RAINBOWS AND COLOR AND LIGHT...

WHAT CAN IT BE?°°

NOTE: THE NEXT TIME YOU USE THIS EXERCISE THE LEADER CAN INVENT VARIATIONS ON THOSE SUGGESTED ABOVE. THE PRIMARY OBJECTIVE IS TO SUGGEST MANY DIFFERENT CATEGORIES OF THOUGHT TO STIMULATE

flexible thinking

NOW TALLY (COUNT) UP YOUR SCORE FOR FLEXIBILITY. HOW MANY NEW IDEAS DID YOU GET THE SECOND TIME THAT YOU DIDN'T THINK OF IN THE FLUENCY EXERCISE? DISCUSS WHY YOU THINK THESE SCORES WERE DIFFERENT IF THEY WERE?

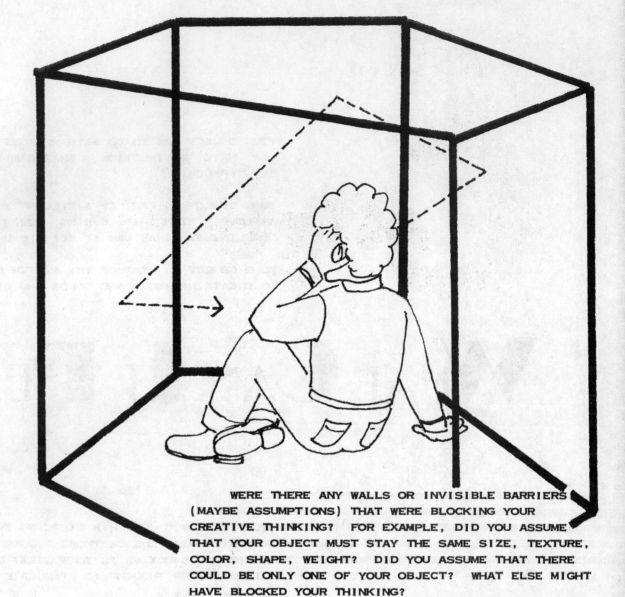

WERE THERE ANY WALLS OR INVISIBLE BARRIERS (MAYBE ASSUMPTIONS) THAT WERE BLOCKING YOUR CREATIVE THINKING? FOR EXAMPLE, DID YOU ASSUME THAT YOUR OBJECT MUST STAY THE SAME SIZE, TEXTURE, COLOR, SHAPE, WEIGHT? DID YOU ASSUME THAT THERE COULD BE ONLY ONE OF YOUR OBJECT? WHAT ELSE MIGHT HAVE BLOCKED YOUR THINKING?

YOU MIGHT LIST WAYS OF BREAKING THROUGH THESE LIMITING ASSUMPTIONS OR CATEGORIES FOR BRAIN-STORMING IDEAS TO STIMULATE FLEXIBILITY IN FUTURE THINKING EXERCISES.

AN ADD-ON
LIST...

CATEGORIES
for BRAINSTORMING

FOOD	TRANSPORTATION
LIQUID STATE	FUTURISM
FROZEN STATE	MUSIC, ART, THEATRE, DANCE
GASEOUS STATE	INDUSTRY
MELTING	BIOLOGY
SMALLER THAN	ASTRONOMY
LARGER THAN	FANTASY
MANY UNITS	MYTHOLOGY
ONLY PART OF	CARTOGRAPHY
GROWING	TOYS
EVOLUTION	TOOLS
ECOLOGY	HOLIDAY TRADITIONS
....	....
....	....
....	....
....	....
....	....

If You Were Riding On The Tip Of A Mouse Whisker...

What kinds of things would you see? Where would you go? How would you keep from falling off? Can you show places you might go and how the world might look if you were so very small and looking up at everything? What might be frightening that you take for granted now (such as a vacuum cleaner)?

life learning, Point-of-View Problem Solvi

THIS IDEA MIGHT LEAD TO A LEARNING EXPERIENCE RAISING QUESTIONS REGARDING POINT-OF-VIEW. FOR EXAMPLE, WHY IS IT IMPORTANT THAT EACH OF US CLEAN OUR PLACE AT THE LUNCH TABLE BEFORE WE LEAVE? THE POINT-OF-VIEW OF ONE PERSON HAVING TO CLEAN UP AFTER MANY PEOPL IS MUCH DIFFERENT THAN THAT OF A PERSON WHO LEFT A MESS WITHOUT CONSIDERING WHO WOULD HAVE TO CLEAN UP AFTER HIM OR HER.

history

WHY WOULD TWO BROTHERS CHOOSE OPPOSITE SIDES TO FIGHT FOR DURING A CIVIL WAR, OR IN A POLITICAL ELECTION?

social studies

WHY DO WE HAVE WARS? WHY DO WE DISAGREE WITH FRIENDS? CAN YOU THINK OF A CURRENT EVENT WHERE BOTH SIDES SEEM TO HAVE A VALID POINT (FROM YOUR POINT-OF-VIEW) AND YET THEY ARE OPPOSING EACH OTHER?

science

A SWAMP MIGHT BE A TRAVEL BARRIER TO A WAGON TRAIN BUT A WELCOME SIGHT TO AN ALLIGATOR BEING PURSUED BY A HUNTER.

literature

WILD THINGS MIGHT BE SCARY OR FINE FRIENDS, DEPENDING UPON HOW YOU CHOOSE TO RELATE TO THEM. A SMALL BOY NAMED MAX LEARNED TO BE "IN CHARGE" OF SCARY DREAMS INSTEAD OF LETTING THEM RULE HIM IN THE BOOK, WHERE THE WILD THINGS ARE BY MAURICE SENDAK.

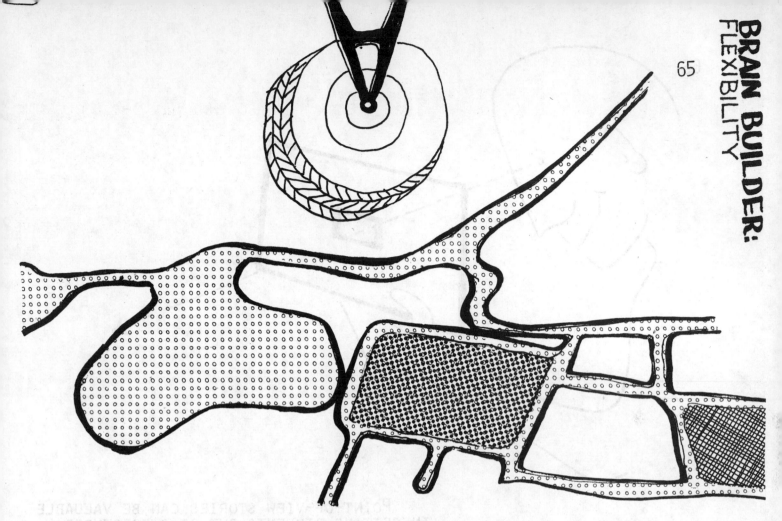

WHAT IF YOU WERE A WHEEL OF AN AIRPLANE?

How would the colors look flashing by on the ground? The designs of the land and highway below are called ground pattern.

You might cut a one inch square out of a piece of paper and use the resulting hole as a view finder. (See opposite side for instructions.) Go on a walk and look for unusual things most people would overlook. Can you find interesting patterns in the broken concrete, details of a car, shadow patterns on a building that look different when isolated? You might collect two or three ideas to combine into an original composition of imaginary ground pattern.

66

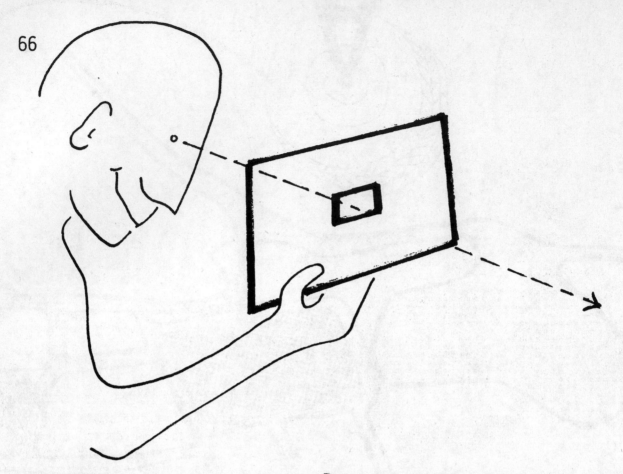

POINT-OF-VIEW STORIES CAN BE VALUABLE
IN GETTING STUDENTS OUT OF STEREOTYPED
HABITS OF THINKING. OFTEN AT CERTAIN AGES,
STUDENTS WILL CONTINUE TO REPEAT THE SAME
TYPE OF PICTURES SUCH AS RACE CARS, AIR-
PLANES OR HORSES. WHEN THIS HAPPENS A
STUDENT MIGHT BE URGED TO EXPLORE THESE
VISUAL IMAGES FURTHER THROUGH THE FOLLOWING
KINDS OF QUESTIONS:

What if you were a wheel of an
airplane? How would the colors
look flashing by on the ground?

OR

How would a horse protect itself
from rain, wind, wolves? How
would a group of running horses
look if you were above them in
a helicopter?

OTHER EXAMPLES OF POINT-OF-VIEW PICTURES
MIGHT BE:

What if you were small enough to
swim in a raindrop or large
enough to use the world as a
marble?

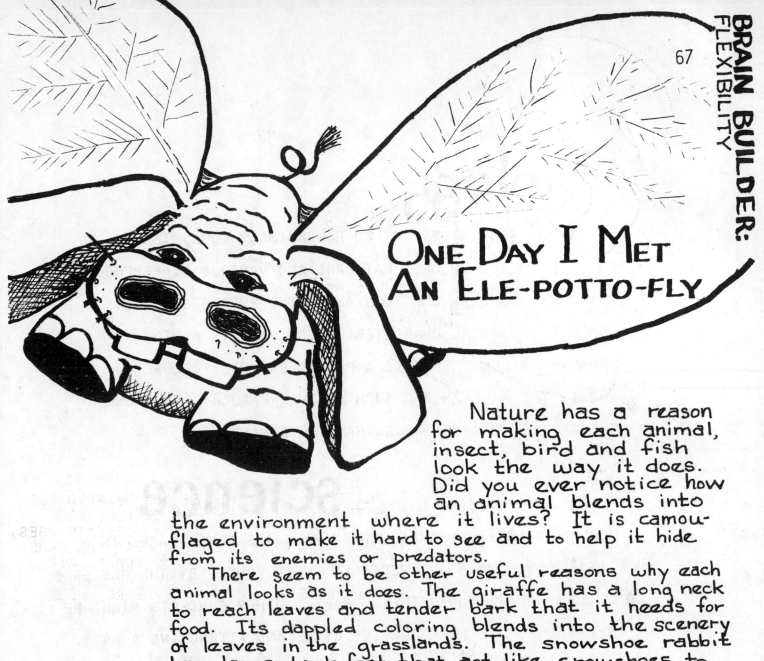

One Day I Met An Ele-potto-fly

Nature has a reason for making each animal, insect, bird and fish look the way it does. Did you ever notice how an animal blends into the environment where it lives? It is camouflaged to make it hard to see and to help it hide from its enemies or predators.

There seem to be other useful reasons why each animal looks as it does. The giraffe has a long neck to reach leaves and tender bark that it needs for food. Its dappled coloring blends into the scenery of leaves in the grasslands. The snowshoe rabbit has large back feet that act like snowshoes to keep it from sinking into deep snow. Large ears pick up sounds of approaching danger and white fur blends into snow.

If you could magically cause fur to grow longer, shorter, become stiff or curly or change colors... or make any other changes, what might happen? Choose an animal, insect, fish or bird. Think of ways to change its appearance and think of reasons for the change. You can use logic or fantasy.

biology

IN DRAWING ATTENTION TO HOW ANIMALS LOOK, THEIR FUR, FEATHERS, COLORS, PATTERNS AND VARIOUS DIFFERENCES, CHILDREN MIGHT BE LED TO EXAMINE THE PURPOSES OR OUTCOMES OF PHYSICAL CHARACTERISTICS. WHY IS A LION BROWNISH YELLOW? WHY IS A PARROT BRIGHTLY COLORED? WHY IS THE MALE ANIMAL SUCH AS THE PEACOCK OFTEN MORE DECORATIVE IN APPEARANCE THAN THE FEMALE?

CONCEPTS FROM UNITS IN **science** CAN BE RELATED SUCH AS HOW ANIMALS ARE CAMOUFLAGED IN THEIR ENVIRONMENT, ESPECIALLY THEIR YOUNG, BY THE PATTERNS, COLORS AND TEXTURES THEY "WEAR". OTHER CONCEPTS MIGHT BE RELATED TO THE REPRODUCTIVE CYCLE AND ATTRACTING A MATE.

SOME BOOKS TO ENRICH THESE TOPICS ARE:
SILENT SPRING BY RACHEL CARSON
THE FISHES
THE MAMMALS
THE INSECTS, LIFE NATURE LIBRARY, TIME INC.

No Two Alike

Just as each person is unique, no two snowflakes are alike. Each snowflake or crystal of snow usually has six repeating parts and would fit within a hexagon, a six-sided figure with equal sides. Can you design a new snowflake pattern? How many can you design with no two alike?

Can you think of a way to create a hexagon design by using scissors, tissue paper and a cutting process?

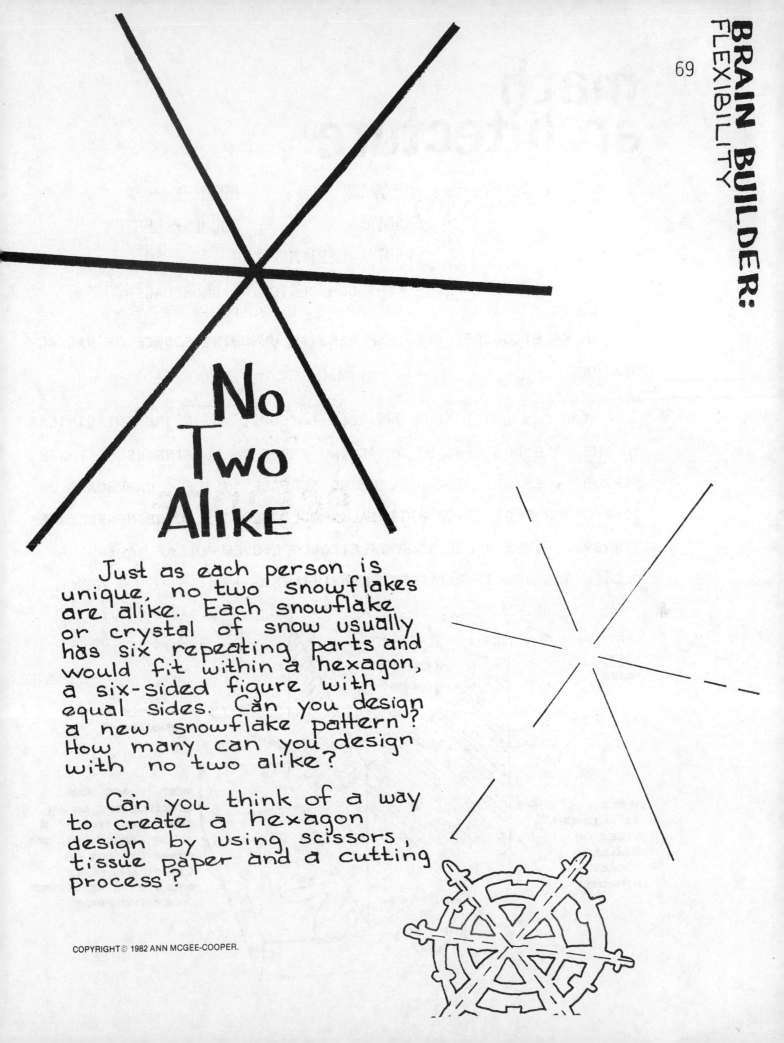

math architecture

CONCEPTS OF: HEXAGON   MODULES

RADIAL   MODULAR DESIGN

RADIAL DESIGN

CAN BE EXPLORED THROUGH DESIGNING SNOWFLAKES.

A KALEIDOSCOPE ALSO EXPLORES AN UNENDING SOURCE OF RADIAL DESIGNS.

YOU CAN BUILD YOUR OWN TELEIDOSCOPE, AN INSTRUMENT SIMILAR TO THE KALEIDOSCOPE, BY ATTACHING THREE SMALL MIRRORS OR THREE MIRROR TILES WITH THE REFLECTING SURFACE INSIDE. CARDBOARD OR SOME OTHER PROTECTIVE MATERIAL SHOULD BE USED TO REINFORCE THE MIRRORS. THEN PLACE YOUR TELEIDOSCOPE OVER A LEAF, A BUG, A FLOWER AND SEE IT REFLECTED MANY TIMES.

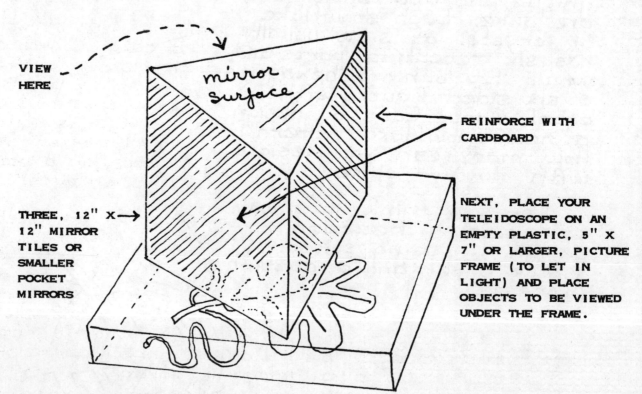

VIEW HERE

mirror surface

REINFORCE WITH CARDBOARD

THREE, 12" X 12" MIRROR TILES OR SMALLER POCKET MIRRORS

NEXT, PLACE YOUR TELEIDOSCOPE ON AN EMPTY PLASTIC, 5" X 7" OR LARGER, PICTURE FRAME (TO LET IN LIGHT) AND PLACE OBJECTS TO BE VIEWED UNDER THE FRAME.

A Peanut Butter and Jellyfish Sandwich

People who fish sometimes hook unexpected catches such as an old boot or even an auto tire. This unsuspecting person will be greatly surprised when she sees what she has caught. Could it be a suitcase full of goldfish, a lifejacket being worn by an octopus, or a peanut butter and jellyfish sandwich?

Can you think of something to draw on the hook that probably has never before been hooked? What will you think of to draw or design? Do lots of brainstorming to generate many possible ideas before you choose one to draw or build. You could build it as a junk sculpture or make a magazine collage.

science ecology

This activity might lead any number of ways into a science unit such as the study of:

- bivalve and univalve shells
- barnacles and other marine crustaceans
- symbiotic relationships between animals

Oceans and rivers have been used as a dumping grounds for a long time. This activity might move from a playful approach to unexpected objects being "fished" out of the sea to a serious study of how careless dumping can harm the balance of nature and lead to pollution.

A delightful book to stimulate the imagination is ▸ McELLIGOT'S POOL BY DR. SEUSS

NOW LET'S EXERCISE

Elaboration

SKILLS

ELABORATION – THE NUMBER OF DIFFERENT
DETAILS USED IN WORKING
OUT AN IDEA.

Little-known facts about well-known Fairy Tales

1. FOR THIS ACTIVITY DIVIDE INTO GROUPS OF
    FOUR TO SIX PEOPLE.

2. EACH GROUP SHOULD CHOOSE AN OBJECT TO
    STIMULATE ELABORATE THINKING.

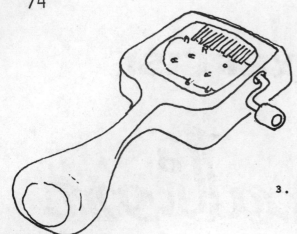

ITEMS SUCH AS A HAND-WOUND MUSIC BOX, A CAN
OPENER, A SKATE KEY, A POTATO PEELER...ANY
UNUSUAL AND INTERESTING OBJECT WILL WORK FINE.

3. EACH GROUP DECIDES WHO WILL START THE EXER-
   CISE. PERHAPS THE STARTER WILL BE:

   - THE PERSON WITH THE MOST HAIR

   - THE PERSON WEARING THE MOST RED

   - THE SHORTEST PERSON

   - THE YOUNGEST PERSON

   - THE PERSON WITH THE LONGEST TONGUE

4. THE STARTER CHOOSES A FAIRY TALE AND BEGINS
   TO TELL LITTLE KNOWN FACTS LINKING THE FAIRY
   TALE TO THE GROUP'S OBJECT.

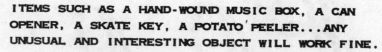

FOR EXAMPLE: SUPPOSE THE OBJECT FOR YOUR
GROUP WAS... _ _ _ _ _ _ _ _ _ _ _ _ →
THE STORY MIGHT BEGIN, "MOST PEOPLE HAVE
HEARD THAT CINDERELLA HAD GLASS SLIPPERS.
BUT FEW PEOPLE HAVE EVER KNOWN WHY. ACTUALLY,
CINDERALLA HAD A BAD AND CONTINUING PROBLEM
WITH ATHLETE'S FOOT FROM THE TIGHT BOOTS SHE
WORE WHEN DOING ALL HER CHORES. NOW HER FAIRY
GODMOTHER KNEW THAT VITAMIN D FROM THE SUN'S
RAYS WOULD KILL THE FUNGUS THAT CAUSED THE
ITCH. SO SHE MADE CINDERELLA'S SLIPPERS
TRANSPARENT TO ALLOW THE VITAMIN D TO SHINE
THROUGH TO CURE HER ITCHY TOES.

NOW WHEN THE HANDSOME PRINCE LEARNED OF THIS
INGENIOUS IDEA, HE...

5. AN NOW IT IS THE NEXT GROUP MEMBER'S TURN TO
    ELABORATE AND ADD "LITTLE KNOWN FACTS" TO THE
    STORY. SINCE THESE FACTS ARE LITTLE KNOWN,
    ANY OUTRAGEOUS AND ORIGINAL IDEA THAT COMES TO
    MIND CAN BE ADDED TO THE STORY. IT HELPS TO
    BE FAMILIAR WITH THE FAIRY TALE. BUT IF A
    GROUP MEMBER HAS NEVER HEARD OF THE FAIRY
    TALE, ENCOURAGE HIM/HER TO JOIN IN AND ADD
    "LITTLE-KNOWN FACTS" AS THEY SEEM TO FIT.
    SOMETIMES NOT KNOWING THE FAIRY TALE CAN MAKE
    THE NEW STORY MORE ORIGINAL.

6. CONTINUE GIVING EACH MEMBER A TURN UNTIL ALL
    HAVE ADDED DETAILS TO THE STORY. IF A GROUP
    REALLY GETS WARMED UP, THEY MAY GO AROUND
    MORE THAN ONCE.

7. TAPE RECORDERS MIGHT BE USED TO RECORD THE
    STORIES. IT CAN BE LOTS OF FUN TO ADD SOUND
    EFFECTS AND SPECIAL VOICES TO THE STORIES,
    TO HAVE SPONSORS AND COMMERCIALS LIKE A RADIO
    SHOW. (ALL THESE ARE VARIATIONS ON THE
    ELABORATION SKILLS AND CAN STRENGTHEN AND
    ENHANCE THE MOTIVATION OF THE GROUP.)

NOTE: This activity can be applied to
any subject area in the curriculum. For
example: You might use little known facts
about well-known events in history or
about well-known rules of punctuation.

ANOTHER ACTIVITY TO STIMULATE ELABORATION IS CALLED

Fairy Tales & the 5 Senses

1. THIS ACTIVITY MOVES MUCH AS THE FIRST ONE DID WITH EACH PERSON IN THE GROUP TAKING A TURN.

2. EACH MEMBER IN THE GROUP CHOOSES ONE OF THE SENSES TO LINK TO THE STORY.

   - SEEING
   - HEARING
   - SMELLING
   - TASTING
   - TOUCHING

   . . . YOU MIGHT ADD ESP.

3. A NEW LEADER CHOOSES A FAIRY TALE OR NURSERY RHYME AND BEGINS TO TELL A STORY. AS THE LEADER GETS TO A PART OF THE STORY WHERE A DETAIL ABOUT ONE OF THE SENSES CAN BE ADDED, THAT PERSON SIGNALS THE LEADER, OR THE LEADER JUST PAUSES WHILE HIS/HER TEAMMATE ADDS THE DETAIL OR ELABORATION.

FOR EXAMPLE:

(LEADER) "FEW PEOPLE CAN APPRECIATE HOW
DELICIOUS AND MELT-IN-YOUR-MOUTH WERE THE
GOODIES PACKED IN RED RIDING HOOD'S BASKET."
(PAUSE FOR PERSON DESCRIBING TASTE TO TAKE
OVER.) "FIRST THERE WERE CRISP RAISIN AND
CHOCOLATE COOKIES WITH GOOEY APRICOT CENTERS.
THE SANDWICHES WERE ON SWEDISH RYE BREAD WITH
CHILLED GOOSE LIVER, FRESH TOMATO SLICES,
CRISP LETTUCE AND CREAMY MUSTARD. THERE WERE
TWO JUICY PEARS, RIPENED TO PERFECTION..."
(THAT PERSON MIGHT STOP TO INVITE THE TEAM
MEMBER DESCRIBING SMELLS OR TEXTURES TO ADD
DETAILS.)

NOTE: ALTHOUGH SKILLS IN BUILDING CREATIVE
THINKING ARE THE FOCUS OF THIS SECTION, NOTE THE
RICH OPPORTUNITY TO BUILD
vocabulary skills,
verbal expression
AND MANY BASIC communication AND
team work skills

Happy St. Stomach's Day

The other organs of the body are in revolt.

"It just doesn't seem fair," complains the bladder "for the heart to get such good press year after year for being the source of love."

"Yeah! What about the rest of us vital organs?" chimed in the liver. "You couldn't do much loving or anything else without me!"

"I love you with all my stomach! Now that has a nice ring to it," noted the stomach.

"Why not have a St. Stomach Day? How about March 1?"

Your job is to brainstorm a new national holiday to honor one of the body's vital organs or parts. Invent a myth or legend of how this tradition began.

You might tell about its founder. In what country and at what time in history did it begin?

You might link to history or a language you are currently studying but by all means

Elaborate with rich fantasy!

80

WHAT ARE THE FEELINGS THAT ARE EXPRESSED THROUGH THIS HOLIDAY? FOR EXAMPLE:

HALLOWEEN	DEALS WITH	SUPERSTITION
THANKSGIVING	-	APPRECIATION
JULY 4TH	-	PATRIOTISM
CHRISTMAS, CHANUKAH	-	GIVING, SHARING

WHAT FOODS ARE PART OF THE TRADITION? HOW AND WHY? WHAT MIGHT BE ESPECIALLY PREPARED FOR THIS DAY (LIKE COLORED EGGS FOR EASTER)? LIST A SCHEDULE OF EVENTS FOR YOUR CELEBRATION IS IT LINKED TO:

PLAY	-	APRIL FOOL'S DAY
HISTORY	-	MEMORIAL DAY
A SPECIAL GROUP IN SOCIETY	-	LABOR DAY?

DOES IT INVOLVE THE GOLDEN WHEAT GRASSHOPPERS IN IOWA OR EARLY CYAFIN HUMONOIDS FROM THE PLANET OF BURP? BRAINSTORM AND DESIGN YOUR ORIGINAL HOLIDAY AND PRESENT A SKIT SHOWING HOW IT IS CELEBRATED.

foreign language

social studies

YOU MIGHT WANT TO RESEARCH THE CUSTOMS AND HOLIDAYS OF OTHER SOCIETIES AND PERIODS IN HISTORY TO GET IDEAS FOR THIS ACTIVITY.

BOOK OF DAYS BY THE NATIONAL GALLERY
BOOK OF DAYS BY KATE GREENAWAY

A SPECIAL KEY THAT GUARDS A SECRET

This key opens a special lock that opens a carefully guarded secret door. The secret isn't gold or jewels. Only you know the secret. Is it a magic cookie machine or a magic garden? Or is it a secret laboratory with special tools and chemicals? Show your idea in a secret drawing.

You might want to fold your paper so that the top of the page could be the door or the lid of a box or a safe. On the inside of the folded page you can show the hidden surprise.

history

science

Secrets and hidden messages have long been a source of fascination. You might want to look up information on the ROSETTA STONE which provided a key to ancient Egyptian writing. Ancient indian pictographs hold many other carefully guarded secrets to past life and knowledge.

There are several formulas that you might use to make secret messages and invisible writing. You can use either lemon juice or milk to write or draw on white paper. Then the receiver holds the paper close enough to a flame to darken the lemon juice or milk being careful not to burn the paper, and soon the hidden message appears.

Another process that is lots of fun is to mix water with one of the "instant brighteners" found in many laundry soap powders. (These are the blue crystals that are mixed with the white powder.) Mix about 1 cup of soap powder to one gallon of water. Then use as a paint with any brush on white butcher paper or newsprint.

Next, find a room that can be closed to become completely dark. Use one or more black lights and watch in amazement as the words and drawings glow brightly in the dark.

You might look up the journals of Leonardo di Vinci, who wrote backwards, perhaps to keep his ideas confidential. The Morse Code, flag signals and crypto-graphs are other ways secrets have been communicated.

This arrow leads to a NEW RAPID TRANSIT SYSTEM

Does it send you upstairs, downstairs or into a tunnel? Do small cars, long trains or slick capsules zip you from place to place? Is it the blood stream that races red corpuscles from your big toe to your nose or is it an underground system that chinch bugs rip around inside devouring the roots of the grass? Design your own special rapid transit system and name it after yourself or invent a name.

The CAROL HUNTING CORPUSCLE EXPRESS.

urban studies

career development

This activity might lead into a unit on community helpers or on urban problems. It might be developed to emphasize all the many career possibilities related to rapid transit, city planning and other community services.

This could be a sneaky way to lead into a study of the circulatory system of the body. A lot of rote learning could be accomplished in the course of labeling pretend streets and avenues (veins and arteries) if this rapid transit system utilized the human blood streams.

Many words could be introduced and/or reinforced, such as

VEHICLES
RAPID TRANSIT
SYSTEMS
CIRCULATORY
VEINS
ARTERIES
CORPUSCLE
KILOMETER

vocabulary

Some interesting stories: THE LITTLE ENGINE THAT COULD BY WATTY PIPER

MARVIN K. MOONEY WILL YOU PLEASE GO NOW! BY DR. SEUSS

HOW LITTLE LORI VISITED TIMES SQUARE BY AMOS VOGEL

Help Wanted!
Flea Circus Lost All Fleas

This is a flea-less flea circus as all the fleas rushed off to lunch on a passing German shepherd. Who took their place on the high wire? What kind of ferocious insects would they tame? What other death-defying acts can you invent?

Think of kitchen tools, small items found around the house like hair pins, rubber bands and bandaids.

Think of rides in an entertainment park.

How can you link these two groups of ideas?

A hair dryer might make a dandy wind tunnel to propel sail planes across a lake in a saucer.

A hand egg-beater might be ridden by a frog as a unicycle act. What zany linking can you imagine?

reading

Some delightful stories to expand awareness of circus life and events are:

CIRCUS BY BRIAN WILDSMITH (ALMOST ALL PICTURES)

IF I RAN THE CIRCUS BY DR. SEUSS

CIRCUS IN THE MIST BY BRUNO MUNARI

THE GIANT ALEXANDER AND THE CIRCUS BY FRANK HERRMAN

CALDER'S CIRCUS: A COLLECTION OF PLAYFUL SCULPTURE BY THE AMERICAN ARTIST, ALEXANDER CALDER.

creative dramatics

A circus can be great fun for role playing and creative dramatics. Playing different performers and animals, creating the movements and gestures of clowns, acrobats and various animals can expand a child's awareness, expression and creative ability.

music

CARNIVAL OF ANIMALS BY CHARLES CAMILLE SAINT-SAENS provides good background music to set a circus mood.

AL KIDWELL IS A DALLAS ARTIST WHO MAKES TOYS AS ART.

Inspiring ORIGINALITY

ORIGINALITY - THE NUMBER OF
STATISTICALLY INFREQUENT IDEAS
THAT SHOW CREATIVE IMAGINATION.

ORIGINALITY IN THINKING MEANS THE ABILITY
TO GENERATE IDEAS DIFFERENT FROM THOSE THOUGHT
OF BY MOST OTHER PEOPLE. THIS THINKING SKILL
IS TRICKY BECAUSE OFTEN IT HAPPENS BEST WHEN
YOU AREN'T TRYING TO DO IT.

88

INSTEAD, IF YOU WORK TO BUILD YOUR SKILLS AT

fluency,

FLEXIBILITY,

and *Elaboration*

THEN OFTEN, SCATTERED IN THE MIDST OF ALL
THOSE MANY IDEAS ARE THE GEMS...

THOSE NOT LIKE ANYONE ELSE'S,

THOSE UNUSUAL,

OFF-THE-WALL,

OUTRAGEOUS,

Original ideas!

JUST TO BECOME MORE AWARE OF ORIGINALITY AS A CHARACTERISTIC OF CREATIVE THINKING, YOU MIGHT:

1. USE THE BRAINSTORMING PROCESS. (SEE PAGES 39 THROUGH 44.)

2. BRAINSTORM IDEAS FOR ONE OF THE FOLLOWING BRAIN BUILDERS:

INVENT A NEW CURE   PAGE 91

A NEW USE FOR A ZIPPER   PAGE 93

THIS POCKET IS FOUND
IN A FUNNY PLACE   PAGE 95

3. STRIVE FOR

fluency,
FLEXIBILITY,
AND *Elaboration*

IN YOUR THINKING.

4. NOW EXAMINE YOUR IDEAS AND DECIDE WHICH ARE THE MOST ORIGINAL OR THE LESS LIKELY TO SHOW UP ON THE LIST OF ANOTHER GROUP BRAINSTORMING THE SAME EXERCISE.

✳ CLUE:

IF YOU GET ANY GREAT IDEAS AFTER
YOU'VE WORKED ON AN EXERCISE (LIKE WHEN
YOU ARE WALKING HOME OR TAKING A SHOWER)
<u>WRITE THEM DOWN</u>!

DR. ROLLO MAY IN HIS BOOK, <u>THE</u>

<u>C</u>OURAGE TO <u>C</u>REATE,

NOTES THAT OFTEN OUR MOST CREATIVE IDEAS

 FROM OUR

SUBCONSCIOUS MIND LATER WHEN WE SEEM TO BE
THINKING OF SOMETHING ELSE.

Rx Patient _____
Doctor _____

PRESCRIPTION:

A YEAR'S SUPPLY OF HICCUPS

You be the doctor and invent a new cure. Will it be a bottle of feathers to tickle a certain grouchy friend and bring on a smile? Or will it be a collection of fuzzy striped caterpillars who will knit fuzzy socks for cold feet? Maybe a year's supply of hiccups could be labeled, "Set time dial on each hiccup to the time you wish to wake up. Then swallow several of these specially timed hiccups." Who can possibly oversleep when a good case of hiccups get going?

**life
learning**

In a society that may look all too often to a pill to solve a problem, it might be constructive to extend this activity by suggesting that problems can be solved in other ways. You might discuss signs of stress and practice methods of relaxation to prevent temper tantrums and tension headaches BEFORE THEY HAPPEN!

One of my favorite gifts to a friend who is worried is a bottle of my own special DUCK OIL. I put baby oil or vegetable oil in any clean, empty bottle. A few drops of food coloring make it interesting. Then I add a fancy label that says something like..."Keep handy. Apply when problems begin to worry you so that they will run right off your worrier just like water off a duck's back."

vocabulary...

PHARMACY

PRESCRIPTION

PHARMACOLOGY

**home
safety**

Some examples of useful home safety rules might be:

1. Keep all medicine out of the reach of small children.

2. Never take medicine that has not been prescribed for you.

THINK OF A NEW USE FOR A ZIPPER.

Maybe it zips up the split in a banana split or a mouth that talks too much or a kangaroo's pocket when mama hops too fast so baby won't spill out. Or maybe it zips a baby bird into a nest or it zips the sky closed after a rain and lightning storm. Or could lightning be a giant zipper that lets the rain out of the sky? What if a highway could be unzipped to go in two directions? A friend of mine invented a PEOPLE ZIPPER that helped people on different sides of an argument to understand each other's difference of opinion and get back together cooperatively. What can you invent as a new use for a zipper?

DESIGN YOURSELF! BY HANKS, BELLISTON, EDWARDS, PUBLISHED BY WILLIAM KAUFMANN, INC.

science

ZIP! ZIPPER! ZIPPING! could playfully lead into science. How does a snake "unbutton" its skin when it is time to shed its skin? What if a butterfly could neatly unzip its cocoon when it was time to emerge? What would happen if the butterfly did not have to struggle and push hard with its muscles? Is this necessary to prepare the butterfly for flight? If so why?

What if baby birds and chickens could neatly unzip their egg shell when ready to hatch? How could you recycle the shell for other uses?

TIME-LIFE SCIENCE LIBRARY
MR. WIZARD'S SCIENCE SECRETS BY DON HERBERT
THE ASCENT OF MAN BY J. BRONOWSKI
IN DEFENSE OF NATURE BY JOHN HAY

THIS POCKET IS FOUND IN A FUNNY PLACE

Is it worn by a fish or a furry creature? Or is it on a piece of furniture? Maybe it's part of a plant or vegetable. It might be large enough for a whole city to hide safely inside. Or it might be so tiny that it could hold a spare pair of wings for a flea.

Imagine new uses for a pocket. Imagine new locations and new owners. Then think of an interesting way to communicate your idea. You might try writing a riddle. For example:

What snaps securely, carries a spare case of measles and is attached to the saddle blanket of a nightmare?

science

Can you think of pockets in nature?

What about

A CAVE

AN AIR POCKET

KANGEROO POUCHES

A VENUS FLY TRAP?

Is a flower pod a seed pocket?

Is a honey comb in a beehive a honey pocket?

Does a female fish have an egg pocket?

What other satchels, suitcases, nooks, containers in

nature can you think of?

language arts

WISHES, LIES AND DREAMS is a delightful book and

record by Kenneth Koch teaching children to write poetry.

WATERSHIP DOWN BY RICHARD ADAMS is a book about

the fascinating underground world of rabbits filled with

tunnels and secret chambers.

THE HOBBIT AND LORD OF THE RINGS BY J. R. R. TOLKIEN

JONATHAN LIVINGSTON SEAGULL AND ILLUSIONS BY

RICHARD BACH. Both of these books would appeal to an

older student, grade seven and up. Both deal with the imagina-

tion as the leading edge of our potential.

"Nothing much happens without a dream. For something

great to happen, it takes a really great dream."

Robert Greenleaf

ALEX F. OSBORN AND OTHERS WHO HAVE DONE
EXTENSIVE RESEARCH ON THE CREATIVE PROCESS
NOTE THAT

EVALUATION

SHOULD BE THE

FIFTH CHARACTERISTIC OF CREATIVE THINKING. ONCE
YOU'VE GENERATED ALL THESE

FLUENT,

FLEXIBLE,

ELABORATE AND

ORIGINAL IDEAS, NOW YOU NEED TO

Make Some Choices!

MANY TIMES
Our best ideas
get lost
BECAUSE:

1 WE DON'T THINK THEY ARE IMPORTANT SO WE DON'T TELL ANYONE, OR. . .

2 WE ARE AFRAID WE MIGHT BE WRONG, OR. . .

3 SOMEONE MIGHT LAUGH, OR. . .

4 IT SOUNDS SO RIDICULOUS, OR. . .

5 IT WILL COST TOO MUCH MONEY TO BE PRACTICAL (SO DID THE FIRST CAR, FIRST TELEVISION SET AND FIRST COMPUTER), OR. . .

6 IT CAN'T BE DONE (THEY SAID THAT ABOUT THE AIRPLANE AND SAILING AROUND THE WORLD AND THE LAZER BEAM), OR. . .

7 THE MANY OTHER REASONS WE INVENT THAT BLOCK OUR MOST CREATIVE IDEA GENERATION.

EXPAND

the use of

EVALUATION

to spot and trigger

Originality.

Use ORIGINALITY as the criteria.

This is an IDEA EVALUATOR MACHINE...

input ideas here

these are criteria wheels

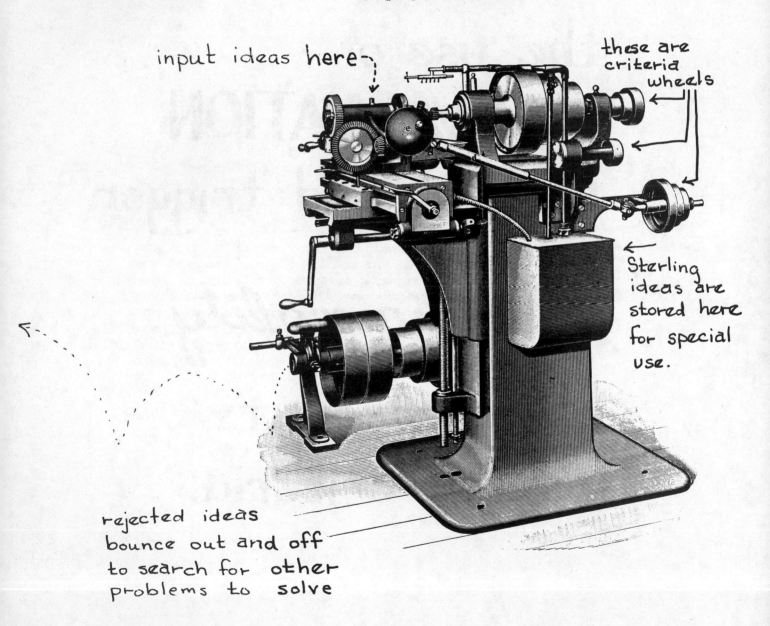

Sterling ideas are stored here for special use.

rejected ideas bounce out and off to search for other problems to solve

BUT ONCE WE'VE GOTTEN THE IDEAS FLOWING
AND RECORDED, NEXT WE NEED TO DECIDE WHICH IDEAS
HOLD THE MOST PROMISE. IT IS IMPORTANT TO KEEP
YOUR MIND OPEN AND LOOSE EVEN IN THIS PROCESS
BECAUSE OFTEN THE SEEDS OF THE MOST PROMISING
IDEA LIE WITHIN SOMETHING THAT SEEMS TO BE ONLY
A FUNNY COMMENT. FOR EXAMPLE, WHEN DR. PAUL
TORRANCE WAS WORKING WITH A TEAM OF HIGH SCHOOL
STUDENTS TO TEACH THEM CREATIVE PROBLEM SOLVING,
THEY POSED A PROBLEM OF DESTRUCTION IN THE SCHOOL.
A SMALL PERCENTAGE OF THE STUDENTS WERE DESTRUC-
TIVE BUT THE COST FOR REPAIR AFFECTED EVERY
STUDENT. WHAT COULD BE DONE?

"SHIP ALL THE DESTRUCTIVE STUDENTS TO
AUSTRALIA!" SAID ONE OF THE PROBLEM SOLVERS.

"NOW THAT'S THE VERY KIND OF IDEA THAT
MIGHT SLIP PAST US ALL AS ONLY AMUSING BUT HAVING
NO REAL PRACTICAL VALUE," SAID DR. TORRANCE.

IN THE NEXT FEW HOURS HE LED THE TEAM OF
STUDENTS THROUGH A PROCESS TO REFINE THE IDEA
UNTIL IT WAS A CREATIVE AND PRACTICAL IDEA.
THE FEW DESTRUCTIVE STUDENTS WOULD BE ISOLATED
IN ONE SCHOOL (INSTEAD OF SHIPPED AWAY) SO THAT
THEY WOULD BE MORE AWARE OF THE EFFECT OF THEIR
DESTRUCTIVE BEHAVIOR. IN ADDITION, THEY WOULD
BE GIVEN RESPONSIBILITY TO DECIDE WHAT PART OF
THE SCHOOL BUDGET WOULD GET CUT (SUCH AS VENDING
MACHINES, FIELD TRIPS, SPORTS EQUIPMENT, SOUND
SYSTEM) TO COVER THE COST OF REPAIRS FOR SCHOOL
DAMAGE THAT RESULTED FROM THEIR DESTRUCTIVE BE-
HAVIOR. DR. TORRANCE ILLUSTRATED CLEARLY HOW A
SEEMINGLY ONLY HUMOROUS REMARK COULD HOLD THE
SEEDS OF A CREATIVE AND FRUITFUL IDEA.

EVALUATION.

the process of

- -DECIDING
- -JUDGING
- -CHOOSING
- -HARVESTING

THE MAJOR VALUE OF GENERATING MANY IDEAS IS TO HAVE A GREAT MANY OPTIONS FROM WHICH TO CHOOSE. BUT WITHOUT THIS PART OF THE PROCESS, THE HARVESTING IS NEVER DONE.

DECIDING WHICH OF THE MANY IDEAS TO SPEND FURTHER TIME ON,

TO TEST

TO REFINE

TO POLISH

TO FINE TUNE

COMES PARTIALLY FROM LOGICAL CRITERIA

(FOR EXAMPLE: WHICH IS LEAST EXPENSIVE, MOST PRACTICAL, PORTABLE, AVAILABLE, APPLICABLE?) AND PARTIALLY FROM INTUITION (THAT PROCESS WHERE YOU KNOW OR HAVE A HUNCH BUT YOU CAN'T EXPLAIN HOW YOU KNOW.)

HERE ARE TWO BASIC APPROACHES TO EXPLORE WITH

EVALUATION.

 APPROACH 1

START WITH THE IDEAS GENERATED FROM ANY OF THE FOLLOWING BRAIN BUILDERS CODED EVAL- UATION OR ANY OF THE OTHER BRAIN BUILDERS IN THE SERIES.

AFTER MANY IDEAS HAVE BEEN GENERATED, DIS- CUSS LOGICAL CRITERIA FOR SELECTING ONE. YOU MIGHT CHOOSE A CERTAIN PERSPECTIVE. FOR EXAMPLE, WHAT IF YOU WERE AN ADVERTISING AGENCY LOOKING FOR ORIGINAL IDEAS FOR AN AD CAMPAIGN? OR WHAT IF YOU WERE LOOKING FOR ENTERTAINING IDEAS FOR A PARTY?

STATE YOUR REASONS FOR YOUR CHOICE. (THIS HELPS CLARIFY CRITERIA. IF FIVE PEOPLE ARE CHOOSING, EACH PERSON IS LIKELY TO BE USING A DIFFERENT CRITERIA OR YARDSTICK.)

APPROACH 2

A SECOND APPROACH IS TO GIVE YOUR INTUITION AND INNER WISDOM OR HUNCHES ENCOURAGEMENT TO GROW. HOLD OFF LOGICAL REASONING FOR AWHILE TO MAKE TIME TO PURSUE SOME ILLOGICAL, INTUITIVE HUNCHES. YOU MIGHT PURPOSELY CHOOSE AN UNLIKELY IDEA TO PURSUE JUST TO EXERCISE EXPANDING YOUR SELECTION PROCESS.

NOW HONE IN ON YOUR CHOSEN IDEA. REFINE IT, POLISH IT, TEST IT, DEVELOP IT.

FOR EXAMPLE: WHILE BRAINSTORMING WAYS TO IMPROVE SCHOOL ATTENDANCE, ONE STUDENT JOKINGLY SAID, "SERVE 14 FLAVORS OF ICE CREAM AND LET US PLAY MORE." EVERYONE LAUGHED AND WENT BACK TO SCRATCHING THEIR BRAINS...LOOKING FOR A REAL SOLUTION.

AT THE END OF THE SESSION, THIS UNLIKELY SUGGESTION WAS CHOSEN TO REFINE AND TEST. IT PROVED TO BE THE RIGHT IDEA NEEDED TO TURN THE ATTENDANCE AROUND FROM 68% TO OVER 90% PRESENT AT SCHOOL ON FRIDAYS. (THE END OF THE WEEK HAD BECOME A HIGH ABSENTEE TIME AND STATE FUNDS BASED ON ATTENDANCE WERE BEING LOST AS A RESULT.)

AFTER DEVELOPING THE IDEA FROM AN OFF-THE-WALL COMMENT "JUST FOR LAUGHS" INTO AN OPERA-TIONAL PROGRAM. THE FOLLOWING RESULTED:

STUDENTS PLANNED THE FRIDAY LUNCH MENU WHICH INCLUDED EVERYTHING FROM OUTSIDE PICNICS, TO ETHNIC FOOD FESTIVALS RELATED TO UNITS OF STUDY, TO HOMEMADE ICE CREAM AND COOKIE SCULPTURE CON-TESTS. HIGH INVOLVEMENT FROM STUDENTS GENERATED A HIGHLY ENTHUSIASTIC RESPONSE.

AND STUDENT TEAMS TOOK TURNS PLANNING AND LEADING THE CURRICULUM ON FRIDAYS. THE ONLY LIMITATION WAS THAT WHAT WAS PLANNED MUST BUILD

ON SKILLS DEVELOPED DURING THE WEEK.   AS A RESULT:

- FASCINATING OUTSIDE SPEAKERS WERE INVITED,
  SUCH AS ATTORNEYS, CITY PLANNERS, CITY
  COUNCIL MEMBERS, ENVIRONMENTALISTS, UNION
  LEADERS, POETS, ARTISTS, PILOTS, ENGINEERS,
  AND BALLOONISTS.

- A MATHEMATICAL MONSOON WAS FOUR FRIDAYS
  FILLED WITH GAMES, PUZZLES, COMPUTER PRO-
  GRAMMING, CONSTRUCTING ACTIVITIES, AND
  ALL KINDS OF CHALLENGING WAYS TO APPLY
  MATH SKILLS.

- HYSTERICAL HISTORY WERE FRIDAYS WHEN STUDENTS
  WERE GIVEN CERTAIN PERIODS IN HISTORY TO
  INVESTIGATE.   THEN DRAMAS AND GAMES CHAL-
  LENGING A GOOD WORKING KNOWLEDGE OF HISTORY
  FILLED THE DAYS WITH BRAIN-BUSTING FUN FOR
  ALL.

LO AND BEHOLD, SOON MONDAY THROUGH FRIDAY
BECAME MUCH BUSIER, MORE MEANINGFUL DAYS, HONING
IN ON THE SKILLS FOR THE BIG FRIDAY CHALLENGE!

ATTENDANCE WAS UP;

LEARNING WAS UP;

ENTHUSIASM WAS UP;

PARENT SUPPORT WAS UP;

STUDENT INVOLVEMENT HAD NEVER BEEN
HIGHER;

TEACHER MORALE WAS UP;

'and it all began from someone's humorous comment

THROWN INTO THE DISCUSSION PRIMARILY TO
GET A LAUGH.   BUT IT ALSO GOT HARVESTED!

"THE SEEDS OF TRUTH OFTEN LAY HIDDEN WITHIN A
PLAYFUL, AMUSING COMMENT. EXPECT TO FIND GEMS
OF WISDOM IN UNEXPECTED PLACES."

G. A. ULRICH

opposite
ᴉˢᴉᴅ∩ umop ∀
and backwards

This poor flea has a bad case of dogs! Can you make a funny or ridiculous picture by reversing things, making them upside down or backwards? What if a tire had four cars on it? Perhaps milk has a glass in it? A chicken may get smaller and smaller and then disappear back into an egg. What kind of opposites can you imagine and draw?

Students might develop a list of OPPOSITE words such as:

light	dark
big	little
high	low
fast	slow

This might be used to introduce and/or reinforce the concepts of:

ANTONYM   AND   SYNONYM.

A Thesaurus could be used to rephrase famous quotations such as, "A PENNY SAVED IS A PENNY EARNED" might become "A SMALL SUM OF MONEY CONSERVED IS THE EQUIVALENT TO THE SAME AMOUNT IN SALARY."

Then see if others can guess the famous quote you had in mind. You might give them the number of words in the quote as a clue.

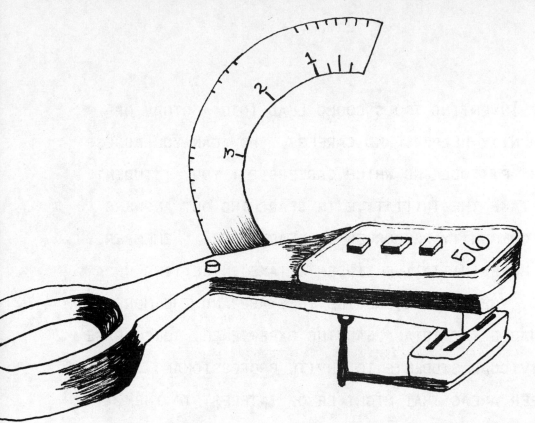

A Thingamajig... or is it a Whatchamacallit?

This is a part of a magic tool that makes everything all right after a very discouraging day. Can you add the other parts and show how the tool works? Think of other tools. Take them apart in your imagination and add parts to this one. Or start from scratch and come up with your all new, handy, dandy _____? Make up a slogan to advertise and sell it.

INVENTING TOOLS COULD LEAD INTO A STUDY OF COMMUNITY HELPERS AND CAREERS. HOW CAN YOU ASSESS YOUR APTITUDE AND WHICH CAREERS FIT YOU? STUDENTS CAN TAKE THE INITIATIVE IN SEARCHING OUT ANSWERS AND COMMUNITY RESOURCES TO LEARN MORE. REMEMBER, THE MORE INITIATIVE STUDENTS TAKE IN SETTING UP A UNIT, THE MORE INTERESTED THEY ARE AND THE MORE VALUABLE THE TOTAL LEARNING EXPERIENCE. ENCOURAGE INDIVIDUAL STUDENTS TO INVITE PROFESSIONALS IN CAREER AREAS THAT MIGHT BE OF INTEREST TO THEM.

INVENTING TOOLS MIGHT LEAD INTO A UNIT ON SAFETY. A GOOD SAFETY REMINDER . . .

A TOOL IS FOR WORK.
A TOY IS FOR PLAY.
PLAYING WITH TOOLS CAN BE DANGEROUS!

A GAME TO INCREASE VOCABULARY AND LANGUAGE SKILLS: HOW MANY TOOLS CAN YOU THINK OF THAT MIGHT BE USED IN

COOKING   SEWING
BUILDING A HOUSE   PAINTING
REPAIRING A CAR   GROWING A GARDEN?

OR PLAY THE GAME ANOTHER WAY AND ONE PERSON NAMES A TOOL, THE NEXT PERSON NAMES THE ENVIRONMENT OR KIND OF PLACE IT MIGHT BE USED.

Commemorating
Vitamin B1 Complex

In Honor of Sir Grover We Gloriously Do Garr!

Design a postage stamp and a coin for a new kingdom. The stamp might be to honor the brave new bean sprouts and the coin to celebrate "king-sized strawberry" in the kingdom of Vigaro Vegetables. What kind of stamps and coins would honor vitamins A and B_1 complex for the kingdom of Drugstore Prescriptions? What kind of stamps might have pets on them? Can you imagine coins with mice, gophers and guinea pigs on them? Or what kind of coins would a colony of earthworms have? Perhaps they'd have an honorary stamp for Sir Grover Grubworm, himself!

112

It can be fun to learn and use new words.

PHILATELY - THE COLLECTION AND STUDY OF POSTAGE STAMPS.

PHILATELIST - ONE WHO COLLECTS POSTAGE STAMPS.

What else would be interesting to collect?

BOTTLE CAPS
POST CARDS
COLORED BOTTLES
DOLLS
BARBED WIRE
SEED PODS
WISHBONES
BROWN-EYED, THREE-TOED CATERPILLARS

Collecting is a way of studying, cataloguing, classifying. This can be a way of developing an awareness and appreciation for the many subtle and varied differences in nature.

From collections of seeds, shells, buttons, twigs, pods, etc., you can enjoy creating a mosaic, a collage or an assemblage by putting things into a new relationship or context.

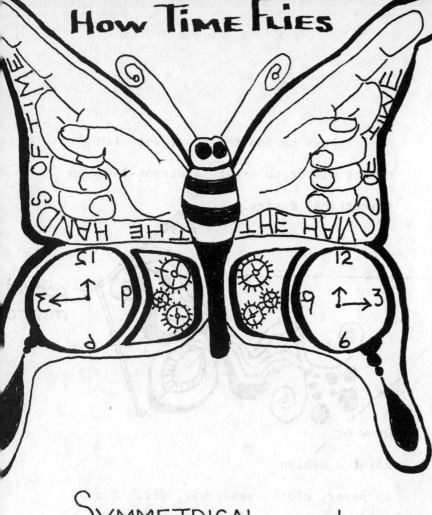

How Time Flies

Synthesizing Symmetrical Design with Nature

SYMMETRICAL - equal arrangement of parts on opposite sides of a plane or line. If folded in half, one side of the design would appear to mirror the other. Can you design your own original insect, fish or bird and make it symmetrical?

*CLUE: Of these two drawings,

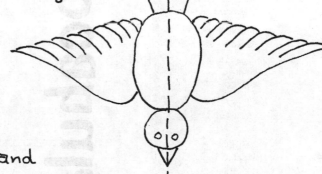

this one is assymmetrical and

this one is symmetrical.

To increase the challenge, think of one or more ideas usually not linked to wildlife and find a way to incorporate this into your design. You might play with names for your new creature searching for puns and synthesized words.

114

It can be fun to experiment with a
pocket mirror to create a mirror-image or
symmetrical design.

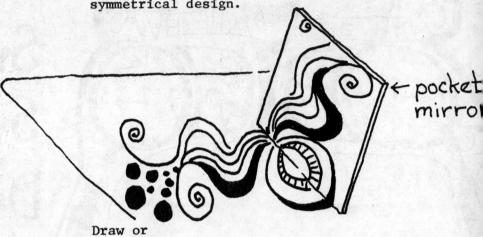

← pocket mirror

Draw or
paint a design
on paper, cloth, sandpaper, etc. Use a
pocket mirror to explore various symmetrical,
repeating images. Try this also with magazine pictures and words. Make a collage or
design fitting several pictures, shapes and
colors together to become a new composition.

Or try this with your full-face, school
portrait. Are both sides of your face
exactly identical opposites? How can you
research this question?

vocabulary

SYNTHESIS	COLLAGE
SYMMETRICAL	ASYMMETRICAL

A delightful book about shapes...
THE WING ON A FLEA BY ED EMBERLEY

THE CARTOGRAPHY OF A FLIRTATIOUS FLEA

Freddie Flea is sending an invitation to his friend, Esmeralda, to meet him for tea this afternoon on the neighbor's St. Bernard dog. He is also enclosing a map so she'll know where to meet him and how to avoid certain dangers along the way such as the toxic flea collar area and the high-wind zone of the tail.

Using a key can you help him make this map? You might include LONGITUDE, latitude (or even SHORTITUDE) markings and elevation symbols. Distance might be measured in flea feet or hops. Would there be mountain ranges and peninsulas or valleys? What other land marks can you imagine? Have fun helping Freddie design this imaginary, nonsense map.

You might draw up a letter of introduction or a love note from Freddie to accompany the map. And if two fleas were having lunch on the ear of a french poodle named Harry, what might be on the menu?

Cocktails might be Bloody Harrys.
Soup d jour might be Cream of Dog Sweat with Crisp, Dog Dandruff Chips.
And for the entre, Filet de Ear, medium rare!

geography

What fun to learn CARTOGRAPHY* from two frivolous fleas! Many of the terms and concepts used in geography, map making and navigation can be introduced, learned, applied and reinforced through problem solving with fantasy maps. A delightful way to evaluate student comprehension of:

ISLAND
PENINSULA
BAY
INLET
RIVER
LAKE
OCEAN
TRIBUTARY

and other geography terms, might be to make an imaginary map showing the vacation route of two dill pickles in a refrigerator using the terms listed above. Applying a word in a new context is an effective way of evaluating the extent of understanding.

* CARTOGRAPHY - ART OR BUSINESS OF DR
OR MAKING CHARTS OR MAPS.

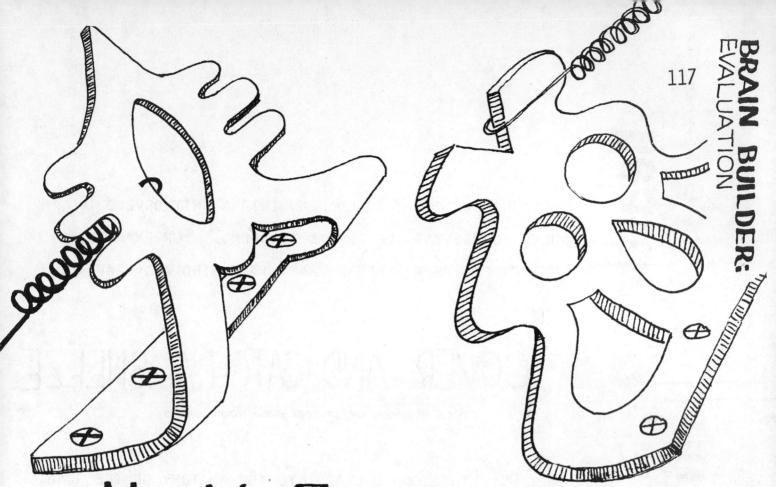

HAVE YOU EVER SEEN A SNEEZE?

Sneezes fly out of us so quickly that few have ever been seen. But one is captured above in this genuine, authentic

SNEEZE TRAP.

Close your eyes and remember as vividly as possible what it's like to sneeze. When and how are you first aware that you might sneeze? Remember the tickle beginning in your nose? Does a sneeze have lots of long legs that tickle your nose hair? Or does it have springs or coils that propel it around in a bouncey motion? Perhaps it has long antennae or wings that cause the tickle. Maybe there is a family of three sneezes sneaking up on you. Or maybe there are different types of sneezes; fierce, shy or gregarious.

Imagine what a sneeze might look like and draw or build a sneeze. You might use feathers, fuzz, yarn, wire or other materials that suggest sneezability.

THIS ACTIVITY COULD LEAD INTO A UNIT DEVELOPING RULES TO PREVENT THE SPREAD OF GERMS. FOR EXAMPLE, A KLEENEX CAN BE A "SNEEZE TRAP" TO REMIND A 5-YEAR-OLD TO

COVER AND CATCH A SNEEZE.

THEN DISPOSE OF IT AND WASH YOUR HANDS.

OR...THIS COULD LEAD INTO THE ANATOMY OF THE NOSE, SINUS, THROAT AREAS IN UNITS ON THE HUMAN BODY.

OLDER STUDENTS MIGHT BE INVOLVED IN THE VOCABULARY OF MICROBIOLOGY SUCH AS:

GERM	ENDOSPORES
VIRUS	FLAGELLA
DISEASE	HANGING-DROP
ALLERGY	PATHOGEN
COCCI	STREPTOCOCCI
SPIRILLIA	

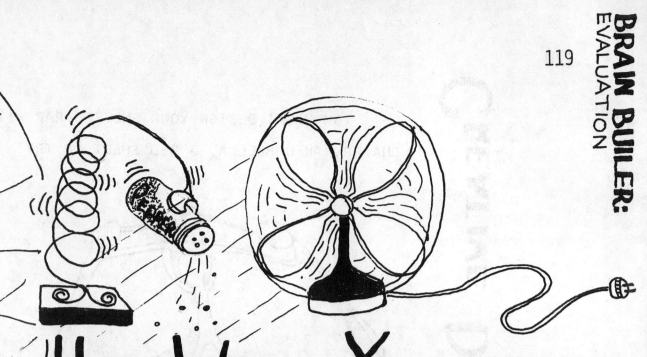

How Would You Bait a Sneeze Trap?

What would entice a sneeze to tiptoe or zoom full speed pell-mell right into a sneeze trap? Does it like damp, chilly, breezy places? Or does it like freshly ground pepper and flower pollen? Or maybe the fragrant aroma of cinnamon and licorice jelly beans would lure a sneeze closer for a curious catapult into your trap.

Design Your Own Sneeze Trap

Would it be a cage, a bubble-like structure, or a giant version of a nasal passage?

CREATIVE DRAMATICS

YOU MIGHT DESIGN YOUR SNEEZE TRAP WITH BOXES, CHAIRS, AN UMBRELLA, A BED SHEET OR TRY

People Sculpture

BRAINSTORM YOUR IDEA AND ARRANGE THE PEOPLE IN YOUR GROUP IN ANY WAY THAT MIGHT SUGGEST A SNEEZE TRAP. THINK OF BODIES AS IF THEY WERE CLAY, WIRE OR OTHER BUILDING MATERIALS. HOW CAN YOU MAKE THE BEST OF THE SPECIFIC ADVANTAGES AND DISADVANTAGES OF BUILDING WITH HUMAN BODIES? YOU WILL WANT TO AVOID ANY ARRANGEMENT THAT MIGHT BE DANGEROUS TO THE PARTICIPANTS. BUT BY BUILDING WITH HUMAN BODIES YOU CAN GIVE YOUR SNEEZE TRAP INSTRUCTIONS AS TO WHAT SOUNDS TO MAKE AND HOW TO MOVE. IT MIGHT START IN A VERY STRETCHED OUT POSITION MAKING A HUMMING SOUND THAT WOULD LURE A SNEEZE INSIDE. THEN IT MIGHT BECOME INCREASINGLY SMALLER UNTIL IT SNAPPED SECURELY AROUND THE SNEEZE WITH A LOUD CLICK!

Now... How Could You Recycle a Sneeze?

First, analyze its properties.
A sneeze has:

Surprise
Sound
Force and Velocity
Wetness
What else?

How could you take each of these properties and recycle it into a new use? For example, could the sound be used in a SNEEZE ALARM SYSTEM? Could the force be used to propel a vehicle such as a two-passenger SNEEZEMOBILE?

Achoo! Achoo! Achoo! Achoo!

ECOLOGY

BRAINSTORM YOUR OWN ORIGINAL IDEAS FOR
RECYCLING A SNEEZE. USE YOUR RIGHT HEMISPHERE AND

BE ZANY AND
COMPLETELY
OUTRAGEOUS . . . .OR. . .SCIENTIFIC

MIX IN A
BIT OF
THEORY AND
LOGIC

REMEMBER...   THE WILDEST, FUNNIEST IDEAS MAY BE
THE FIRST STEP TOWARD A PRACTICAL AND BRILLIANT
NEW DISCOVERY!

DR. BARBARA CLARK, IN HER BOOK, GROWING UP GIFTED, GIVES US A LIST OF

10 ASSUMPTIONS
Guaranteed to Block
creativity!

1. EVERYTHING MUST BE USEFUL.

2. EVERYTHING MUST BE SUCCESSFUL.

3. EVERYTHING MUST BE PERFECT.

4. EVERYONE MUST LIKE YOU.

5. YOU SHALL NOT PREFER SOLITUDE TO TOGETHERNESS.

6. YOU MUST HAVE CONCENTRATED ATTENTION.

7. YOU MUST NOT DIVERGE FROM CULTURALLY IMPOSED SEX NORMS.

8. DO NOT EXPRESS EXCESSIVE EMOTIONAL FEELING.

9. DO NOT BE AMBIGUOUS.

10. DO NOT ROCK THE CULTURAL BOAT.

124

CAN YOU RESTATE THESE INTO POSITIVE SUGGES-
TIONS OF TEN WAYS GUARANTEED TO NURTURE CREA-
TIVITY? (THIS WOULD BE A GOOD ACTIVITY FOR A
SMALL GROUP OR FOR A CLASS TO DEVELOP. THE RESULTS
COULD BE POSTED AS A DAILY REMINDER TO ALL.)

FOR EXAMPLE, THE FIRST THREE ASSUMPTIONS
MIGHT BE RESTATED AS FOLLOWS:

1. ALLOW A PLACE IN YOUR THINKING FOR FANTASY AND
FOOLISHNESS, FOR THESE ARE THE SEEDS OF GREAT IDEAS
TO COME.

2. FAILURE IS AN IMPORTANT PART OF LEARNING.
YOU MUST BE WILLING TO MAKE LOTS OF MISTAKES IN
ORDER TO UNCOVER YOUR BEST IDEAS. A MISTAKE IS
NEVER A LOSS UNLESS YOU FAIL TO LEARN FROM IT.

3. PERFECTION IS NOT EVERYTHING. CHOOSE SOME TIMES
TO PURPOSELY NOT BE PERFECT. SOME SUPER IDEAS
CAN BREAK THROUGH WHEN YOU LOOSEN UP AND RISK.

DISCUSS THE OTHER ASSUMPTIONS AND WHY THEY
BLOCK CREATIVITY. HOW WOULD YOU RESTATE THEM?
YOU MIGHT WANT TO RESTATE THE FIRST THREE
ASSUMPTIONS IN YOUR OWN WORDS.

CONCEPTUAL REPATTERNING

or Creative Problem Solving

CREATIVE PEOPLE TYPICALLY TURN THEIR PROBLEMS INTO OPPORTUNITIES. WHILE OTHER LESS CREATIVE PEOPLE COMPLAIN AND FRET ABOUT HOW BAD THINGS ARE, THE CREATIVE PROBLEM SOLVER GETS AROUND ON ALL SIDES OF THE PROBLEM UNTIL S/HE FINDS A WAY TO MAKE IT WORK AS A POSITIVE RATHER THAN A NEGATIVE. FOR EXAMPLE, WHEN A RESEARCHER CAME UP WITH A SMELLY MESS THAT PRODUCED CLOUDS OF UGLY BLACK SMOKE INSTEAD OF THE RESULTS HE EXPECTED, RATHER THAN WALKING AWAY WITH A SENSE OF FAILURE, HE BEGAN TO ANALYZE THE CHARACTERISTICS OF WHAT HE HAD PRODUCED. WE NOW ALL DEPEND DAILY UPON HIS FAILURE-TURNED-INTO-AN-OPPORTUNITY...AND CALL IT RUBBER.

LET'S GO SLOWLY THROUGH THE STEPS OF THIS PROCESS. ONE OF THE PRIMARY BLOCKS TO SEEING AND FINDING NEW SOLUTIONS IS RIGID THINKING. THE ABILITY TO SEE THINGS FROM MANY PERSPECTIVES IS ESSENTIAL. CONCEPTUAL BLOCKBUSTING IS AN IDEA OF JAMES L. ADAMS THAT EMPHASIZES THE NEED TO BREAK APART OLD IDEAS OR CONCEPTS. SINCE TO ME BLOCKBUSTING SUGGESTS BEING BLOWN TO BITS OR POSSIBLY DESTROYED FOR FURTHER USE. I PREFER THE TERM,

Conceptual Repatterning

step 1.

IT WORKS LIKE THIS:

DEFINE THE PROBLEM AS CLEARLY AS POSSIBLE. YOU MIGHT DRAW IT, OR DESCRIBE IT IN WORDS. BUT GET SOMETHING DOWN ON PAPER.

step 2.

step 3.

NOW BREAK THE PROBLEM INTO PARTS.
WHAT ARE THE CAUSES OF THE PROBLEM?
WHAT OR WHO MIGHT BE POSSIBLE RE-
SOURCES?

PLAY WITH NEW POSSIBLE LINKS. TURN
THE PIECES OF THE PROBLEM AROUND AND
LOOK AT DIFFERENT WAYS TO FIT THEM
TOGETHER. WHO NEEDS THE SOLUTION TO
THE PROBLEM? WHO WOULD BENEFIT
BY CONTRIBUTING TO THE SOLUTION
OF THE PROBLEM?

WE OFTEN MAKE THE MISTAKE OF GOING TO
SOMEONE AND SAYING, "I NEED YOU TO
HELP ME WITH MY PROBLEM." INSTEAD,
WE MIGHT SEARCH FOR A SITUATION WHERE
WE COULD HONESTLY SAY, "YOU CAN BENEFIT
IN THIS WAY BY PROVIDING THIS RESOURCE
FOR ME."

FOR EXAMPLE: A HIGH SCHOOL MATH TEACHER
WANTED PRIZES FOR AN ANNUAL MATH MARA-
THON, AN EVENT SHE DREAMED UP TO MOTIVATE
STUDENTS TO SHARPEN AND INCREASE THEIR
MATH SKILLS. SHE FIRST APPROACHED HER
PRINCIPAL WITH A PLEA OF, "I NEED YOUR
HELP!" "SORRY, NO MONEY LEFT IN THE
BUDGET," HE REPLIED.

NEXT SHE TRIED THE APPROACH OF THINKING
WHO MIGHT BE HELPED BY PROVIDING
PRIZES. SHE WENT TO MERCHANTS IN HER
SCHOOL NEIGHBORHOOD WHO MARKETED ITEMS
OF INTEREST TO HER STUDENTS AS POTENTIAL
CUSTOMERS. HER APPROACH WAS, "I CAN HELP
YOU ATTRACT MORE CUSTOMERS TO YOUR BUSI-
NESS IF YOU WILL PROVIDE A PRIZE FOR THE
ANNUAL MATH MARATHON. YOUR PRIZE WILL
ADVERTISE TO ALL THE STUDENTS YOUR
PRODUCT AND LOCATION."

SHE GOT MORE PRIZES THAN SHE HAD EVER IMAGINED. AND NOW, SEVERAL YEARS LATER, THE MERCHANTS ACTUALLY CALL HER TO BE SURE THEY GET INCLUDED.

step 4.

THE FIRST THREE STEPS HAVE BEEN DONE WITH THE BRAIN IN BETA OR FOCUSED THINKING. NOW SHIFT GEARS MENTALLY AND PUT THE PROBLEM ASIDE. PURPOSELY FORGET IT. GO TO SOMETHING ELSE. AS DR. ROLLO MAY DESCRIBES IN HIS BOOK, THE COURAGE TO CREATE, THE

Eureka!

OR CREATIVE SOLUTION MOST OFTEN BUBBLES UP WHEN THE BRAIN IS IN ALPHA (A DAY DREAM STATE) OR NOT CONSCIOUSLY THINKING ABOUT THE PROBLEM. SO OFTEN WHEN TAKING A WALK, DRIVING HOME, TAKING A SHOWER OR DOING SOME ROUTINE "NO-THINK" TASK, THE SOLUTION TO A PROBLEM WE HAVE BEEN WORKING ON SUDDENLY SEEMS TO POP INTO OUR MIND. WHEN THIS WILL HAPPEN CAN NOT BE PREDICTED, BUT UNTIL IT DOES, ROTATE BACK AND FORTH BETWEEN FOCUSED CONCENTRATION ON THE PROBLEM (BETA) AND RELAXED TIME AWAY FROM THE PROBLEM, PLAY OR DAY DREAMING (ALPHA). THIS WORKS LIKE TILLING THE SOIL. FARMERS HAVE LONG KNOWN THAT BY TURNING OVER THE FARM LAND EACH YEAR THE SOIL BECOMES MORE PRODUCTIVE AND FERTILE. IN THE SAME WAY BY ROTATING BACK AND FORTH BETWEEN ALPHA AND BETA THINKING, THE THOUGHTS OF THE BRAIN ARE "TURNED OVER" ALLOWING FOR MORE FERTILE AND PRODUCTIVE LINKING AND PRODUCTION OF NEW THOUGHT COMBINATIONS.

128

step 5. BE PLAYFUL, PURPOSELY PLAY WITH
NONSENSE, OUTRAGEOUS IDEAS! THIS
LOOSENS UP TIGHT THINKING AND CREATES
A CLIMATE MORE PERMISSIVE TO CREATIVE,
UNUSUAL IDEAS. REMEMBER THAT ANY
REALLY NEW IDEA WILL SEEM OUTRAGEOUS
AT FIRST GLANCE.

Eureka! WHEN THE LIGHT FLASHES,
THEN...

step 6. TEST YOUR NEW IDEA. TRY IT OUT.
EXPECT TO MAKE CHANGES.

step 7. REFINE YOUR IDEA AS NEEDED. WHEN
GEORGE DE MESTRAL GOT THE BRIGHT IDEA
FOR VELCRO BY CAREFULLY OBSERVING
HOW THE BURDOCK BURR STUCK FAST TO ANY
WOVEN FABRIC, IT TOOK HIM EIGHT YEARS
AND COUNTLESS EXPERIMENTS TO REFINE HIS
IDEA INTO THE EFFICIENT MATING NYLON
TAPES NOW IN SUCH WIDE USE.

A FAMOUS AMERICAN INVENTOR USED TO PUZZLE HIS
ASSISTANTS BY WELCOMING THEIR REPORTS OF BAD
NEWS WITH, "OH, GOOD!" WHILE THEY AGONIZED
OVER THE RECENT FAILURE HE WOULD GO INTO HIS
OFFICE OR LAB AND SEARCH FOR A WAY TO MAKE
THE NEWS GOOD.

MANY PEOPLE AVOID NEW IDEAS BECAUSE THEY
DON'T LIKE CHANGES. BUT ANY NEW IDEA WILL
NECESSITATE CHANGE. EXPECT IT. MAKE IT WORK
<u>FOR YOU</u> RATHER THAN <u>AGAINST YOU</u>. THE
KEY TO THIS IS

EXPECT THE RESULTS TO BE POSITIVE AND THEY WILL
BE. PROFESSOR ROBERT K. MARTIN, PSYCHOLOGIST
AT COLUMBIA UNIVERSITY, EXPLAINS THIS IN HIS
RESEARCH ON THE PYGMALION EFFECT AND THE
SELF-FULFILLING PROPHECY. THE EXPECTATION
OF THE EVENT CAN ACTUALLY CAUSE IT TO HAPPEN.
WE LOOK FOR WHAT WE EXPECT TO HAPPEN. WHEN WE
FIND EVIDENCE TO SUPPORT OUR EXPECTATION WE
WELCOME IT. WHEN WE FIND EVIDENCE TO THE CON-
TRARY, WE USUALLY DISCOUNT IT.

FOR EXAMPLE, IF WE EXPECT TO BE A POOR SPELLER WE SAY, "OH I CAN'T SPELL CAT!" THEN IF WE SURPRISE OURSELF AND OTHERS BY SPELLING WITH ACCURACY, WE SAY, "OH I WAS JUST LUCKY" OR, "THEY MUST HAVE GOTTEN MY PAPER MIXED UP WITH SOMEONE WHO IS A GOOD SPELLER." AND SURE ENOUGH, WE GRAVITATE BACK TO OUR "EXPECTED" LEVEL OF PERFORMANCE.

SO, EXPECT YOUR PROBLEMS TO BE OPPORTUNITIES...WAITING TO BE DISCOVERED.

CONCEPTUAL REPATTERNING (ANOTHER WAY OF SAYING CREATIVE PROBLEM-SOLVING) CAN BE SEEN MORE CLEARLY PERHAPS THROUGH THE FOLLOWING EXERCISE.

1. SELECT A PIECE OF PAPER OR CARDBOARD AND THINK OF IT AS DEFINING YOUR PROBLEM/OPPORTUNITY.

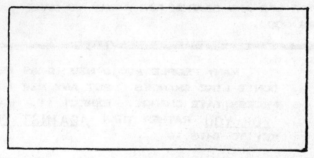

2. CUT IT INTO PUZZLE PIECES. THINK OF THIS AS ANALYZING YOUR PROBLEM OR BREAKING IT UP INTO SMALL MORE MANAGEABLE PIECES.

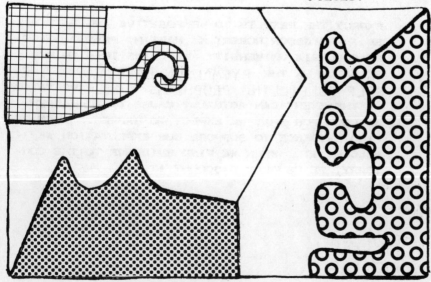

3. NOW LOOK FOR NEW WAYS TO COMBINE THE
    PIECES.   THIS IS MUCH LIKE CLOUD
    WATCHING WHERE YOU PLAY, "WHAT CAN IT
    BE?" WITH THE SHAPES AND COMBINATIONS
    OF SHAPES.

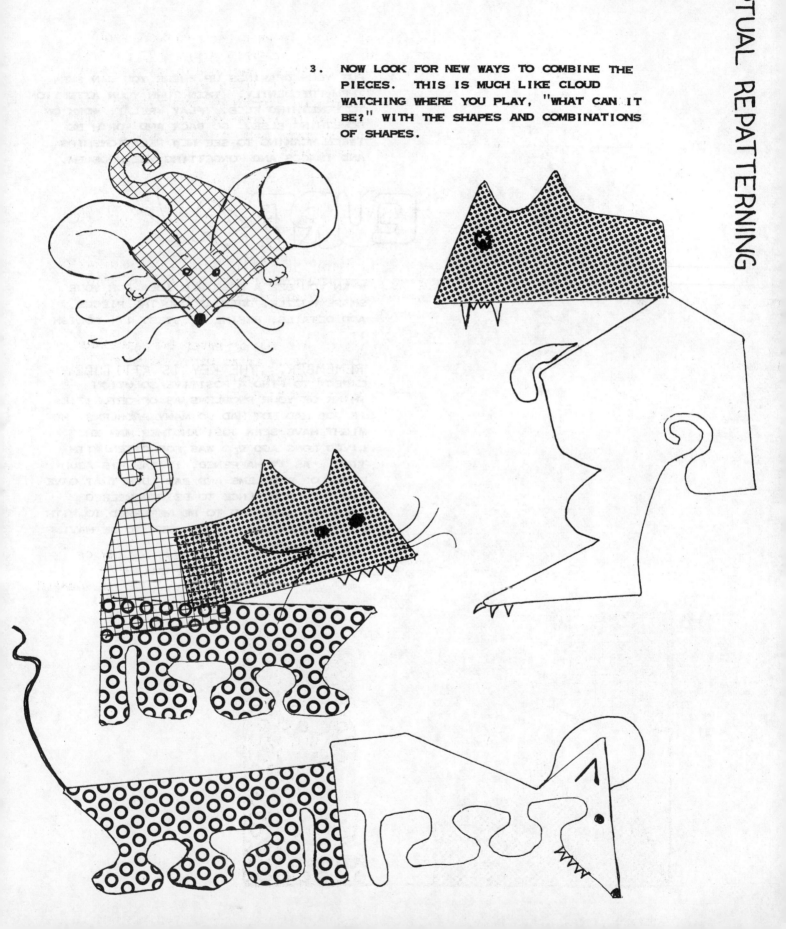

4. PUT YOUR DRAWINGS UP WHERE YOU CAN SEE THEM FREQUENTLY. THEN TURN YOUR ATTENTION TO SOMETHING ELSE. PLAY, RELAX, WORK ON SOMETHING ELSE. GO BACK AND FORTH BETWEEN WORKING TO SEE NEW RELATIONSHIPS AND IMAGES AND FORGETTING THE PROBLEM.

5. WHEN YOU SEE A POSSIBLE IDEA FOR YOUR SHAPE PUZZLE, DRAW AROUND THE PIECES, ADD DETAILS, REFINE IT, TEST IT, POLISH IT.

6. REMEMBER...THE KEY IS ATTITUDE. EXPECT TO FIND A POSITIVE SOLUTION. THINK OF YOUR PROBLEMS AS OPPORTUNITIES. IF JOB HAD NOT HAD SO MANY PROBLEMS, HE MIGHT HAVE BEEN JUST ANOTHER MAN WHO LIVED LONG AGO WHO WAS FORGOTTEN WITH TIME. AS IT HAPPENED, IT WAS HIS ABUNDANCE OF PROBLEMS AND BAD LUCK THAT GAVE HIM THE PROMINENCE TO BE REMEMBERED OVER THE AGES AND TO BE REFERRED TO WITH SUCH COMMENTS AS, "YOU SEEM TO BE HAVING ALL THE LUCK OF JOB!"

DEVELOPING PO POWER:
Learning to think in new ways

AFTER SPENDING MANY YEARS STUDYING HOW CREA-
TIVE MINDS THROUGHOUT HISTORY HAVE SOLVED PROBLEMS,
EDWARD DE BONO GIVES US SOME SIGNIFICANT INSIGHTS
IN HIS BOOK, <u>NEW THINK</u>. HE NOTES THAT WHILE WE
PRIMARILY TEACH AND REINFORCE A VERTICAL METHOD
OF THINKING AND PROBLEM-SOLVING, MOST IMPORTANT
CONTRIBUTIONS HAVE COME THROUGH WHAT HE CALLS
LATERAL THINKING. THERE IS A PARALLEL BETWEEN
DE BONO'S CONCEPT OF VERTICAL/LATERAL THINKING
AND THE LEFT/RIGHT BRAIN THEORY.

<u>VERTICAL THINKING</u> (AND LEFT-BRAINED THINK-
ING) IS GOAL ORIENTED. IT IS WORKING TOWARD A
SPECIFIC ANSWER. LOGIC AND RATIONAL THINKING
ARE EMPLOYED TO BLOCK WANDERING OR SEEMINGLY
IRRELEVANT THOUGHTS. VERTICAL THINKING IS DIS-
CIPLINED THINKING. IT CHIEFLY EMPLOYS THE SKILLS
OF THE LEFT HEMISPHERE.

<u>LATERAL THINKING</u> (AND RIGHT-BRAINED THINK-
ING) IS THE OPPOSITE OF VERTICAL THINKING. IT
MIGHT BE THOUGHT OF AS PLAYING AROUND, WASTING
TIME, DAY DREAMING OR WOOL GATHERING. PERHAPS
YOU FEEL SOME DISCOUNTING OF THIS PROCESS EVEN
AS I DESCRIBE IT. WE ARE NOT USUALLY TAUGHT TO
VALUE THIS TYPE OF THINKING AND PROBLEM-SOLVING
AND OFTEN EVEN FEEL GUILTY WHEN CAUGHT AT IT.
YET AGAIN AND AGAIN IN THE RESEARCH ON CREATIVE
PROBLEM-SOLVING WE LEARN THAT IT IS THIS PROCESS
WHICH DE BONO CALLS LATERAL THINKING THAT PRODUCES
THE A-HA'S AND THE EUREKAS...THAT FLASH OF INSIGHT
THAT PRODUCES CREATIVE INSIGHT AND SOLUTIONS.

WHAT IF WE DEVELOPED AN EQUAL APPRECIATION FOR LATERAL THINKING AS WE HAVE FOR VERTICAL THINKING? INSTEAD OF TRYING TO DECIDE WHICH IS BEST, WE STRIVE TO DEVELOP BOTH AS EQUALLY STRONG AND EFFECTIVE SKILLS TO USE IN PROBLEM-SOLVING. ACTUALLY, THE TWO SKILLS COMPLIMENT EACH OTHER. EACH CAN BE USED TO HELP THE OTHER SKILL ALONG ITS WAY. FOR EXAMPLE, WHEN WE GET BLOCKED USING VERTICAL THINKING, DE BONO TEACHES US TO SWITCH TO LATERAL THINKING. USE PLAY AND LET YOUR MIND WANDER. WHEN NOT PUSHING FOR AN ANSWER BUT LETTING THE MIND WANDER AIMLESSLY, MANY TIMES THE MAGIC LINK IS SUDDENLY MADE. AND WHEN IT IS MADE, NOTE THAT USUALLY IT WILL BE USING PROCESSES OF VERTICAL THINKING WITHIN THE LINKING PROCESS.

TO USE ANOTHER ILLUSTRATION, WHEN THE SWISS ENGINEER, GEORGE DE MESTRAL, INVENTED THE VELCRO FASTENER, HE USED LATERAL THINKING OR WOOL GATHERING TO LINK THE NEED FOR A FLEXIBLE FASTENER TO HIS OBSERVATIONS OF A CLINGING BURDOCK BURR. BUT THEN HE USED ALL HIS SKILLS IN VERTICAL THINKING TO LOGICALLY OBSERVE, ANALYZE, EVALUATE, TEST AND REFINE THROUGH COUNTLESS EXPERIMENTS UNTIL, AFTER EIGHT YEARS, VELCRO WAS FINALLY READY TO MARKET.

DE BONO NOTES THAT THE WORD, "NO" PLAYS AN IMPORTANT PART IN KEEPING THE MIND IN THE PROCESS OF VERTICAL THINKING. IF YOU START TO GET SIDE TRACKED OR OFF TARGET YOU SIMPLY SAY, "NO" TO YOURSELF OR OTHERS TO BLOCK THE DIVERSION. FOR EXAMPLE, IF I'M TRYING TO FINISH THIS PARAGRAPH AND YOU INVITE ME TO FLY A KITE WITH YOU, I BLOCK THE DIVERSION BY SAYING, "NO." DE BONO DECIDED

THAT LATERAL THINKING NEEDED THE SAME KIND OF
SHIELD. SO HE INVENTED THE WORD PO. PO IS
USED TO BLOCK DEMANDS TO MAKE SENSE, GET TO
THE POINT, BE PRODUCTIVE. WHEN YOUR OWN INNER
VOICE OR SOMEONE ELSE BEGINS TO INSIST THAT
YOU STOP DAYDREAMING OR PURSUING YOUR GOAL-LESS
LATERAL THINKING, YOU CAN SAY, "PO!" PO SUS-
PENDS THE DEMAND TO BE VERTICAL TO ALLOW MORE
TIME TO THINK IN A LATERAL PROCESS. THIS CAN
BE LOTS OF FUN TO USE THROUGHOUT YOUR DAY.
YOU MIGHT MAKE A POSTER TO REMIND YOU OF BOTH
TYPES OF THINKING AND THE TWO SHIELDS TO
PROTECT YOUR TIME TO PURSUE EACH THINKING
PROCESS.

2x2 DRAWINGS

(Two-Handed Drawings by Two People)

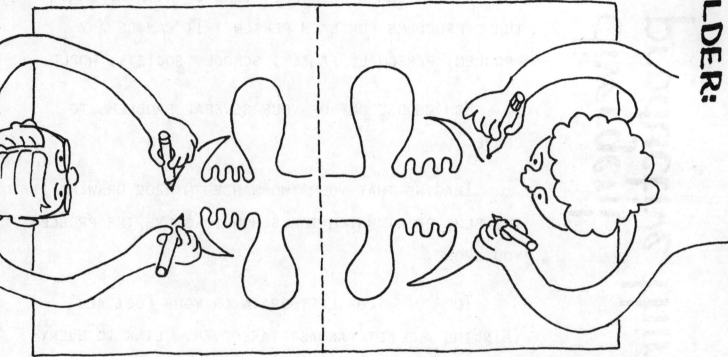

1. Start with a large piece of paper or side of a card board box.
2. Position yourself each at one end of the paper.
3. Imagine a line down the center of the paper between you.
4. Each person should have a paint brush or marker in <u>each hand</u> so that each will be drawing with <u>both hands</u> <u>simultaneously</u>.
5. One person begins the design with both markers at the imaginary center line. What one hand draws is "mirrored" by the other hand.
6. At the same time (so go slowly) your partner begins drawing with both hands <u>mirroring your line</u> on his/her side of the paper. (See above)
7. Then it is your partner's turn to lead with you mirroring his/her line design. Continue taking turns leading and mirroring until the page is filled.

divergent
productive thing

teaming skills

Next:

Brainstorm a problem. Come up with at least three problems for each person. It can be any problem; personal, family, school, society, world.

Now choose one of your several problems to solve.

Imagine that your two-handed mirror drawing is the blue print which tells how to solve the problem you chose.

Turn off your left-brain or your logical thinking and let fantasy take over. Link to everything you can

HOW MACHINES WORK
GAMES
TOYS
TOOLS
SYSTEMS
CURES FOR DISEASES

Let parts of your design suggest ideas to you. Think out loud. Piggyback onto ideas with your partner. Be completely outrageous and playful.

Now begin to add your ideas to the mirror drawing. You might write in directions, for example:

1. Plug into electric current.
2. Input problem.
3. Fan begins to blow warm air over problem.
4. Allow time to incubate.

Or, you might design an owner's manual to accompany the blueprint. Why not write a warranty or instruction book?

Give your new invention a name. Imagine how it was invented. What great problem in the life of the inventor caused him/her to need this solution?

Have fun with the process. Remember,

Creativity links our playfulness with all prior knowledge.

And fun energizes our playfulness.

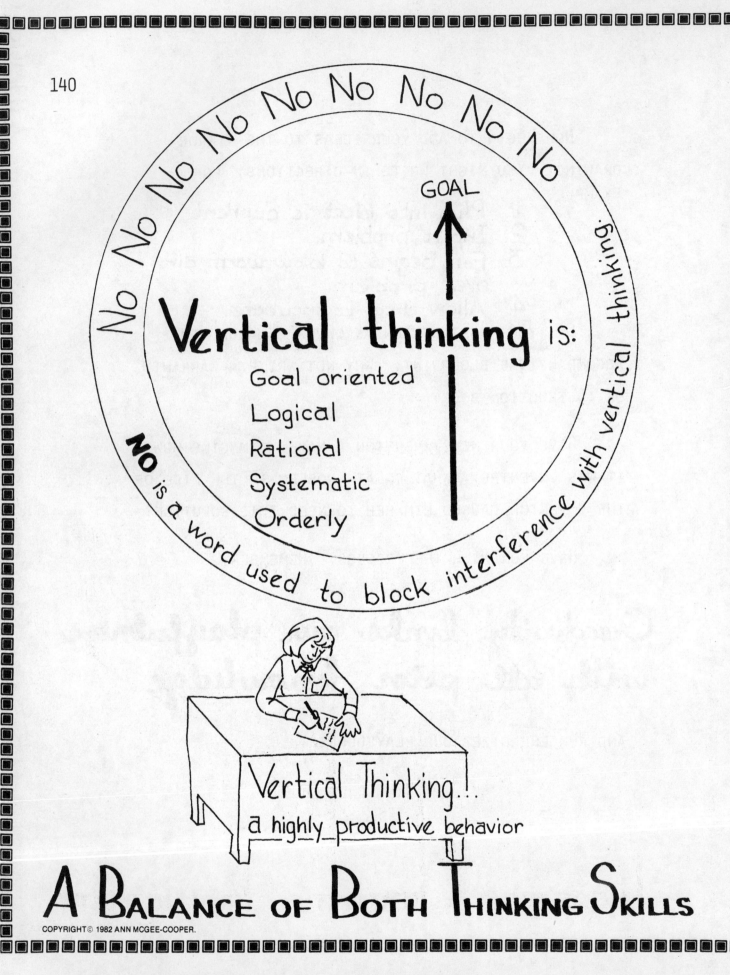

No No No No No No No No

NO is a word used to block interference with vertical thinking.

GOAL

Vertical thinking is:

Goal oriented
Logical
Rational
Systematic
Orderly

Vertical Thinking...
a highly productive behavior

A Balance of Both Thinking Skills

141

Lateral Thinking...
a highly creative behavior

INCREASED CREATIVITY & PRODUCTIVITY

142

"If we could raise the level of creativity of the average person by a small percentage, the social consequences would be very great."

J. P. GUILFORD

GUILFORD, J.P., "CAN CREATIVITY BE DEVELOPED," (REPORTED FROM ART EDUCATION II, JUNE 58,) EDUCATION DIGEST VOL. 24 NO. 4, DEC. 58, PG. 49.

A VOCABULOUS ADVENTURE

or...

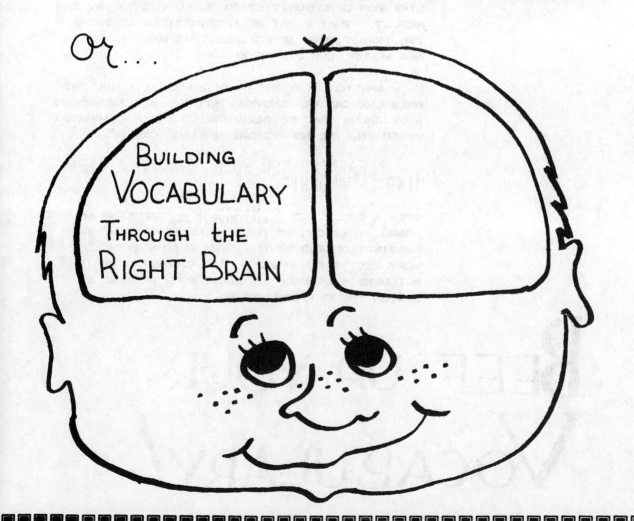

BUILDING
VOCABULARY
THROUGH the
RIGHT BRAIN

BUILDING A DYNAMIC, PERSONAL VOCABULARY IS BASIC TO INCREASING YOUR BRAIN POWER. ONCE YOU HAVE NEW IDEAS YOU WILL NEED TO COMMUNICATE THEM ARTICULATELY AND EFFECTIVELY. GATHERING NEW WORDS IS A WAY TO GATHER IN NEW IDEAS. AS YOU LEARN NEW THINGS YOU WILL AUTOMATICALLY NEED NEW WORDS TO DESCRIBE AND RETAIN ALL THAT YOU ARE LEARNING. IT ALL WORKS TOGETHER. YET UNFORTUNATELY, MANY PEOPLE GET TURNED OFF BY BUILDING NEW VOCABULARY. WHEN IT IS PRESENTED AS A DULL, DRILL OR ROUTINE LESSON,

"HERE ARE TEN NEW WORDS TO LOOK UP AND USE IN SENTENCES,"

IT TURNS OFF BRIGHT MINDS. OR WHEN NEW WORDS ARE PRESENTED IN WAYS THAT INTIMIDATE OR IMPLY THAT THE LISTENER IS DUMB, THEN A GENERAL DIS-LIKE FOR OPPORTUNITIES TO BUILD VOCABULARY CAN RESULT. WHAT MIGHT BE ALTERNATIVES TO THESE TWO TRADITIONAL APPROACHES THAT MAKE LEARNING NEW WORDS SEEM DISTASTEFUL?

WHY NOT PLAY WITH NEW WORDS? IF ALL THE PRESSURE CAN BE REMOVED FROM THE SITUATION AND A GENEROUS DOSE OF PLAYFULNESS AND FOOLISHNESS MIXED IN, THE NON-VERBAL MESSAGE CAN BE,

"LEARNING NEW WORDS CAN BE A NIFTY MIND EXPANDER!"

WHEN A WORD LIKE SINISTRORSE APPEARS ON THE BOARD, THIS CAN BE THE SIGNAL TO WAKE UP YOUR IMAGINATION AND SPRING INTO ACTION WITH YOUR VERY BEST BRAIN POWER. THE FOLLOWING BRAIN BUILDERS WILL HELP INCREASE YOUR ARSENAL OF DELIGHTFUL ENTICEMENTS TO

BEEF UP YOUR VOCABULARY!

Creative people invent new words to name their new ideas. The

telephone,

helicopter and zipper

were all words that were invented to name someone's new idea.

What new words have you invented? Sometimes we accidentally invent a new word. These are all new words invented by friends.

Gription

"Hey Mom, my new tennis shoes have great gription when I run."

Rayo - Age 6

Umpertold

"Oh no! I just umpertold the sugar bowl."

Mary - Age 3

Vocabulous

"That speaker was extremely vocabulous!"

Ann - Age 45

(After reversing procedures in a math problem...)

Lexdypsia

"I've got lexdypsia."

Bruce - Age 63

Ann's Dictionary

You might keep a family, class or personal dictionary to collect words so fresh that they didn't get published in Webster's Dictionary.

Collecting in "Ann's (or whoever's) Dictionary" can give permission to be imaginative with words, can teach how language grows and changes and can encourage a more powerful use of language.

THIS BRAIN BUILDER AND WORD GAME WAS DESIGNED BY SHIRLEY, DAVID, RANDY, MARTHA & CAROL HUNTING

THIS SILIQUOSE SERICIN IS INVITING YOU TO...

1. Locate fun-sounding words in the dictionary, words that are new to you and your peers.

2. Put adjectives on one color or shape of card; put nouns on cards with a different color or shape.

3. Use adj. to code adjective cards and N. to code noun cards.

4. Choose one noun and one adjective card.

5. Using the adjective to describe the noun, create a creature through drawing, sculpture or creative dramatics to convey your idea of these new words.

NOTE: Use your imagination, not the dictionary, to think up a definition. Listen to the word. What ideas does it suggest? Does it sound like another word you know?

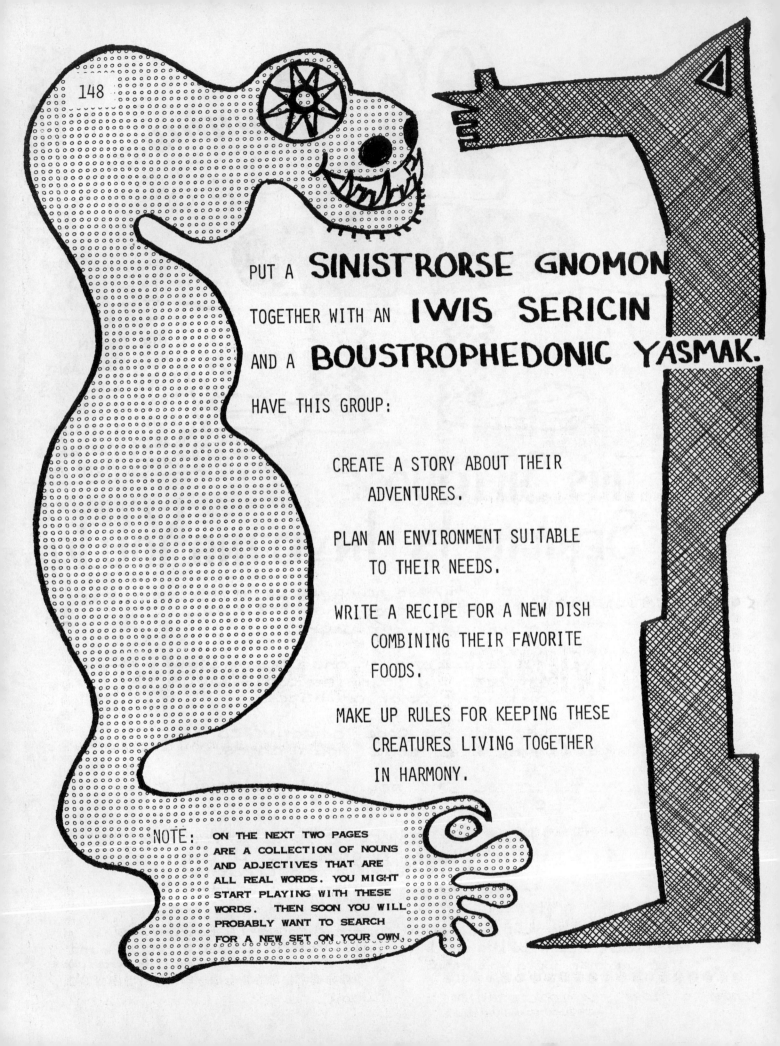

148

PUT A **SINISTRORSE GNOMON** TOGETHER WITH AN **IWIS SERICIN** AND A **BOUSTROPHEDONIC YASMAK.**

HAVE THIS GROUP:

CREATE A STORY ABOUT THEIR ADVENTURES.

PLAN AN ENVIRONMENT SUITABLE TO THEIR NEEDS.

WRITE A RECIPE FOR A NEW DISH COMBINING THEIR FAVORITE FOODS.

MAKE UP RULES FOR KEEPING THESE CREATURES LIVING TOGETHER IN HARMONY.

NOTE: ON THE NEXT TWO PAGES ARE A COLLECTION OF NOUNS AND ADJECTIVES THAT ARE ALL REAL WORDS. YOU MIGHT START PLAYING WITH THESE WORDS. THEN SOON YOU WILL PROBABLY WANT TO SEARCH FOR A NEW SET ON YOUR OWN.

noun

ARDEB

noun

Espadrille

noun

Rhabdomancy

noun

YASHMAK

noun

DUUMVIRATE

noun

AQUARELLE

noun

ENTABLATURE

noun

PORPHYROID

A **Noun** is a word used to name a person, place or thing.

A **Noun** is a word used to name a person, place or thing.

A **Noun** is a word used to name a person, place or thing.

A **Noun** is a word used to name a person, place or thing.

A **Noun** is a word used to name a person, place or thing.

A **Noun** is a word used to name a person, place or thing.

A **Noun** is a word used to name a person, place or thing.

A **Noun** is a word used to name a person, place or thing.

noun...noun...noun

KILDERKIN

noun...noun...noun 151

WEIGELA

noun...noun...noun

YOUNKER

noun...noun...noun...noun

LYCANTHROPE

noun...noun...noun

CONJUNCTIVA

noun...noun...noun

Kermis

noun...noun...noun

Rubric

noun...noun...noun...noun

pyrocatechol

152

A **Noun** is a word used to name a person, place or thing.

A **Noun** is a word used to name a person, place or thing.

A **Noun** is a word used to name a person, place or thing.

A **Noun** is a word used to name a person, place or thing.

A **Noun** is a word used to name a person, place or thing.

A **Noun** is a word used to name a person, place or thing.

A **Noun** is a word used to name a person, place or thing.

A **Noun** is a word used to name a person, place or thing.

ADJECTIVE · ADJECTIVE · ADJECTIVE · ADJECTIVE · ADJECTIVE · ADJECTIVE · ADJECTIVE · ADJECTIVE

XERIC

Oligarchical

SINISTRORSE

Boustrophedonic

Funicular

MERISTIC

Execrable

Omnifarious

154 An __ADJECTIVE__ is a word that describes a noun.

An __ADJECTIVE__ is a word that describes a noun.

An __ADJECTIVE__ is a word that describes a noun.

An __ADJECTIVE__ is a word that describes a noun.

An __ADJECTIVE__ is a word that describes a noun.

An __ADJECTIVE__ is a word that describes a noun.

An __ADJECTIVE__ is a word that describes a noun.

An __ADJECTIVE__ is a word that describes a noun.

ADJECTIVE · ADJECTIVE ·

Proventricular

ADJECTIVE · ADJECTIVE ·

Corticolous

ADJECTIVE · ADJECTIVE ·

FULMINANT

ADJECTIVE · ADJECTIVE ·

ARACHNIDAN

ADJECTIVE · ADJECTIVE ·

Jocose

ADJECTIVE · ADJECTIVE ·

CAMPESTRAL

ADJECTIVE · ADJECTIVE ·

ZYMOLYTIC

ADJECTIVE · ADJECTIVE ·

MESENCEPHALIC

An **ADJECTIVE**
is a word that
describes a noun.

An **ADJECTIVE**
is a word that
describes a noun.

An **ADJECTIVE**
is a word that
describes a noun.

An **ADJECTIVE**
is a word that
describes a noun.

An **ADJECTIVE**
is a word that
describes a noun.

An **ADJECTIVE**
is a word that
describes a noun.

An **ADJECTIVE**
is a word that
describes a noun.

An **ADJECTIVE**
is a word that
describes a noun.

THIS GAME GETS EVEN MORE FUN IF YOU EXPAND IT BY COLLECTING YOUR OWN GROUP OF LITTLE-KNOWN VERBS AND ADVERBS. JUST GET OUT YOUR DICTIONARY AND BEGIN THE SEARCH. NOTICE THAT THE PART OF SPEECH IS LISTED BESIDE EACH WORD.

A TIP TO TEACHERS AND PARENTS:

CHECK YOUR IMPULSE TO ENCOURAGE YOUNGSTERS TO START BY LOOKING FOR THE "REAL" DEFINITION IN THE DICTIONARY. THIS IS YOUR LEFT-BRAIN TAKING OVER. IF YOU WILL ALLOW TIME AND ROOM FOR RIGHT-BRAINED IMAGINATION WITH WORD MEANINGS, YOUNGSTERS WILL GET INTERESTED IN NEW WORDS, WORD ROOTS, HOW THEY ARE FORMED, ETC. ALLOW THE LEFT-BRAINED SKILLS TO BECOME NECESSARY ON THEIR OWN AND THE LEARNING WILL BE MORE PROFOUND.

Joan is an <u>inventigator</u>.

(one who investigates
new inventions)
From a typo by Ruth Lawrence

158

EXPANDING BRAIN POWER
THROUGH <u>BLOOM'S TAXONOMY</u>

DR. BENJAMIN A. BLOOM IN HIS TAXONOMY OF
COGNITIVE THINKING HELPS US UNDERSTAND WHY SO
LITTLE OF THE TOTAL BRAIN'S CAPACITY IS BEING
DEVELOPED AND APPLIED. BELOW YOU WILL NOTE THAT
BLOOM HAS SIX LEVELS OF COGNITIVE THINKING.

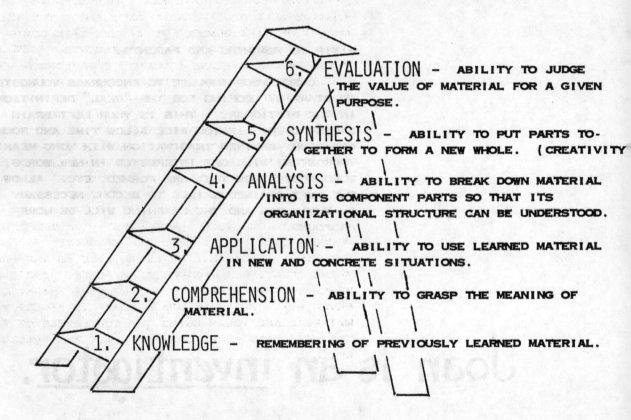

6. EVALUATION - ABILITY TO JUDGE
THE VALUE OF MATERIAL FOR A GIVEN
PURPOSE.

5. SYNTHESIS - ABILITY TO PUT PARTS TO-
GETHER TO FORM A NEW WHOLE. (CREATIVITY

4. ANALYSIS - ABILITY TO BREAK DOWN MATERIAL
INTO ITS COMPONENT PARTS SO THAT ITS
ORGANIZATIONAL STRUCTURE CAN BE UNDERSTOOD.

3. APPLICATION - ABILITY TO USE LEARNED MATERIAL
IN NEW AND CONCRETE SITUATIONS.

2. COMPREHENSION - ABILITY TO GRASP THE MEANING OF
MATERIAL.

1. KNOWLEDGE - REMEMBERING OF PREVIOUSLY LEARNED MATERIAL.

IT IS IMPORTANT TO NOTE THAT THE LEVELS MOVE
FROM THE SIMPLEST AT LEVEL 1 TO THE MOST COMPLEX
AT LEVEL 6. MORE COMPLEX LEVELS OF THINKING
CANNOT BE ACHIEVED WITHOUT UNDERSTANDING
AND APPLYING THE LOWER LEVELS, SO THE HIGHER
ON THE TAXONOMY ON WHICH YOU ARE WORKING, THE
MORE OF THE LEVELS YOU ARE UTILIZING.

IN REVIEWING THIS TAXONOMY WITH TEACHERS AND STUDENTS ALL ACROSS THE NATION, MOST CONFIRM THAT A MAJORITY OF TEACHING IS DONE AT LEVELS 1, 2 AND 3. MOST TESTS APPLY ONLY THE FIRST THREE LEVELS. YET MORE LEARNING IS HAPPENING AT LEVELS 4, 5 AND 6. (ALL OF THE BRAIN BUILDERS DEVELOP LEVELS 4, 5 AND 6.)

IN AN ARTICLE BY ROGER L. HANSON IN "GIFTED/CREATIVE/TALENTED CHILDREN", MARCH/APRIL, 1978, A GRAPH ADAPTED BY IRVING SATO SHOWS THE RELATIVE AMOUNT OF TIME DEVOTED TO LEVELS OF BLOOM'S TAXONOMY BY AVERAGE AND GIFTED STUDENTS. (SEE PAGE 161). BECAUSE AVERAGE STUDENTS TAKE LONGER TO UNDERSTAND AND RETAIN INFORMATION, THEY NEED TO WORK LONGER AT THE FIRST THREE LEVELS. ALSO, THE LEVELS 4, 5 AND 6 CANNOT BE USED WITHOUT A SOLID GRASP OF THE FIRST THREE LEVELS. IN CONTRAST, HOWEVER, GIFTED STUDENTS TYPICALLY GRASP AND RETAIN INFORMATION ON THE FIRST THREE LEVELS RAPIDLY. THEY CAN BE EXPECTED TO LOSE INTEREST UNLESS THEY MOVE ON TO LEVELS 4, 5 AND 6.

NEXT, CONSIDER WHERE CREATIVITY AND CREATIVE PROBLEM-SOLVING FIT INTO THE TAXONOMY OF COGNITIVE THINKING. SYNTHESIS AT LEVEL FIVE IS THE PROCESS WHERE CREATIVE THINKING TAKES PLACE. AND EVALUATION, WHICH IS CHARACTERISTIC OF CREATIVE THINKING, IS LEVEL SIX. BUILDING BRAIN POWER IS FILLED WITH MATERIAL AND IDEAS USING THE TOP LEVELS OF THE TAXONOMY (AND THEREFORE USING ALL THE PRECEDING LEVELS).

IN EDUCATING THE GIFTED STUDENT, WE HAVE LEARNED THAT THE STUDENTS NEED ACCESS TO THE STRATEGIES USUALLY AVAILABLE ONLY TO TEACHERS. BLOOM'S TAXONOMY CAN GIVE BOTH STUDENT AND TEACHER A BETTER UNDERSTANDING AS TO WHY CREATIVITY, HUMOR AND PLAY ARE SO IMPORTANT IN EXPANDING BRAIN POWER. BOTH NEED PERMISSION TO ENJOY THE NATURAL ENERGY AND EXCITEMENT GENERATED FROM THE MORE COMPLEX LEVELS OF LEARNING WHICH SEEMS MORE LIKE FUN THAN THE HARD WORK OFTEN EXPECTED FROM SERIOUS SCHOOL WORK.

STUDENTS AND TEACHERS OFTEN FEEL GUILTY - FEELING THEY NEED TO GET BACK TO THE SERIOUS SCHOOL WORK - WHEN IN FACT THEY ARE MOVING UP TO MORE COMPLEX, CHALLENGING AND THEREFORE APPROPRIATE LEARNING.

BLOOM'S TAXONOMY

TAKEN FROM "GIFTED/CREATIVE/TALENTED CHILDREN" MARCH/APRIL, 1978, P. 31

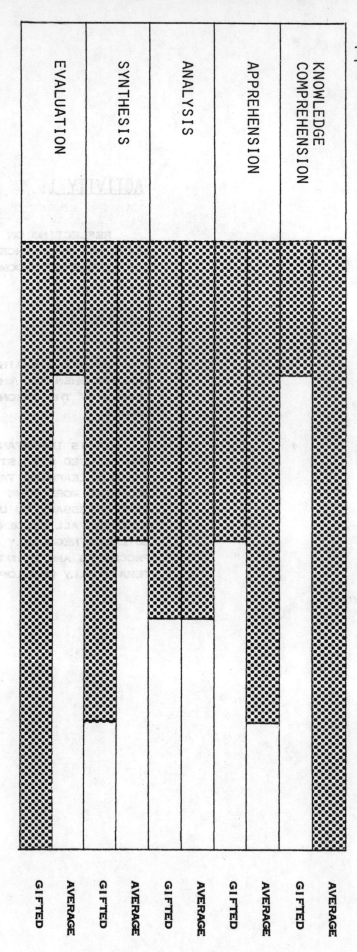

KNOWLEDGE COMPREHENSION

APPREHENSION

ANALYSIS

SYNTHESIS

EVALUATION

AVERAGE GIFTED AVERAGE GIFTED AVERAGE GIFTED AVERAGE GIFTED AVERAGE GIFTED

RELATIVE AMOUNT OF TIME TO BE DEVOTED TO LEVELS OF BLOOM'S TAXONOMY BY AVERAGE AND GIFTED STUDENTS (ADAPTED FROM SATO)

ROGER L. HANSON, CONSULTANT
TALENTED AND GIFTED PROGRAM
LOESS HILLS AREA EDUCATION AGENCY 13
BOX 1109
COUNCIL BLUFFS, IOWA 51502

ACTIVITY 1:

REFLECTING ON YOUR DAY OR WEEK, THINK OF ONE LEARNING EXPERIENCE WHICH WOULD FIT EACH OF THE SIX LEVELS OF BLOOM'S TAXONOMY.

ACTIVITY 2:

SELECT A BRAIN BUILDER YOU HAVE COMPLETED. ANALYZE WHEN AND WHERE YOU USED EACH OF THE SIX LEVELS OF THE TAXONOMY. HAVE A REASON FOR EACH CHOICE.

IT IS IMPORTANT TO NOTE THAT BRAIN BUILDERS CAN BE USED WITH STUDENTS WHO ARE QUICK TO MASTER VARIOUS LEARNING TASKS WHILE AVERAGE STUDENTS, WHO NEED MORE TIME AT LEVELS 1, 2 AND 3, TAKE THE TIME NECESSARY TO UNDERSTAND AND MASTER LEARNING. HOWEVER, ALL STUDENTS CAN BENEFIT FROM USING BRAIN BUILDERS REGULARLY AS MORE OF THE VARIOUS BRAIN PROCESSES ARE BEING CALLED INTO ACTION AND SYS-TEMATICALLY DEVELOPED.

GUILFORD'S STRUCTURE OF INTELLECT

IN CREATIVITY, THE PATTERN IS FOR A PROBLEM TO BECOME AN OPPORTUNITY.   A TYPICAL EXAMPLE IS THE STORY OF THE WORK OF DR. J. PAUL GUILFORD, A MAN WHOSE LIFE WORK HAS MADE A MAJOR CONTRIBUTION TO DISCOVERING AND EXPANDING OUR TOTAL BRAIN POWER.

AT THE BEGINNING OF WORLD WAR II, THE ARMED FORCES HAD A MAJOR PROBLEM.   A SUCCESSFUL WAR EFFORT DEPENDED UPON GETTING A MAXIMUM NUMBER OF MEN TRAINED AS PILOTS, NAVIGATORS AND BOMBADEERS. IN SPITE OF A STRINGENT PROCESS TO SELECT QUALIFIED TRAINEES, THE FAILURE RATE IN THE PROGRAM WAS OVER 30%.   GUILFORD, A PSYCHOLOGIST-STATISTICIAN, WAS CALLED IN TO TASK-ANALYZE EACH OF THE DUTIES AND DEVELOP A SCREENING PROCESS FOR TRAINEES.   WITHIN A YEAR GUILFORD HAD CUT THE FAILURE RATE TO UNDER 10% AND EMBARKED ON A LIFE'S WORK.

IN APPRECIATION FOR A JOB WELL DONE, THE GOVERNMENT FUNDED GUILFORD'S RESEARCH AND DURING THE NEXT TEN YEARS HE AND HIS ASSOCIATES METIC- ULOUSLY ANALYZED MANY ACTIVITIES ON THE JOB AND IN THE CLASSROOM.   FROM THESE FACTOR ANALYTIC STUDIES, GUILFORD PROPOSED A NEW THEORY OF INTELLIGENCE, THE STRUCTURE OF INTELLECT, ALSO KNOWN AS S.O.I.   RATHER THAN AN INTELLIGENCE, GUILFORD PROPOSED THAT THERE ARE 150 DIFFERENT TYPES OF INTELLIGENCE.   HE OUTLINED THREE DIMEN- SIONS OF INTELLIGENCE: CONTENTS OR INPUTS INTO THE MIND; OPERATIONS, THE PROCESSES THE MIND PERFORMS; AND PRODUCTS OR THE RESULTS OF THE THINKING PROCESS.   HE ILLUSTRATED THIS CONCEPT WITH THE CUBE WHICH FOLLOWS:

THE STRUCTURE OF INTELLECT*

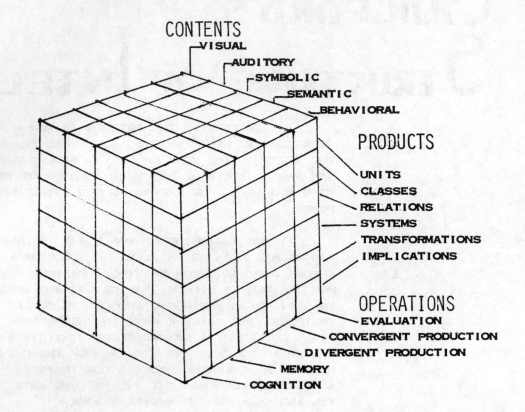

CONTENTS
- VISUAL
- AUDITORY
- SYMBOLIC
- SEMANTIC
- BEHAVIORAL

PRODUCTS
- UNITS
- CLASSES
- RELATIONS
- SYSTEMS
- TRANSFORMATIONS
- IMPLICATIONS

OPERATIONS
- EVALUATION
- CONVERGENT PRODUCTION
- DIVERGENT PRODUCTION
- MEMORY
- COGNITION

DR. MARY MEEKER, A STUDENT OF GUILFORD'S AT U.S.C., BECAME INTERESTED IN THE APPLICATION OF S.O.I. TO TEACHING IN SCHOOLS. OF THE 150 TYPES OF INTELLIGENCE ONLY A SMALL PERCENTAGE ARE TAUGHT IN TRADITIONAL SCHOOLS. AND YET IT HAS BEEN DETERMINED THAT EACH OF THESE TYPES OF INTELLIGENCE CAN BE TAUGHT AND STRENGTHENED. DR. MEEKER HAS DEVELOPED SYSTEMATIC MATERIALS TO TEST AND TEACH THE 150 S.O.I. TYPES OF INTELLIGENCE. FOR FURTHER INFORMATION SHE CAN BE CONTACTED THROUGH THE SOI INSTITUTE WHICH SHE HEADS IN EL SEGUNDO, CALIFORNIA.

* GUILFORD, J.P. WAY BEYOND THE IQ BUFFALO, NEW YORK, CREATIVE EDUCATION, INC., 1977.

THE S.O.I. PROFILE IS A MUCH MORE RELEVANT
INDICATOR OF POTENTIAL THAN THE STANDARD I.Q.
TESTS FOR SEVERAL REASONS (IN FACT MANY NOW
CONSIDER THE STANDARD I.Q. TESTS OBSOLETE).
THESE STANDARD TESTS MEASURE ONLY APPROXIMATELY
FROM 9 TO 44 OF THE 150 TYPES OF INTELLIGENCE
AND THEN AVERAGES THESE INTO A SINGLE SCORE.
IN CONTRAST, S.O.I. GIVES THE LEVEL OF PRESENT
APPTITUDE IN EACH OF 120 AREAS (ONE LEVEL HAS
YET TO BE FACTORED) OR A PROFILE OF ABILITIES.
FROM THIS PROFILE, A TEACHING PLAN CAN BE DE-
SIGNED TO SYSTEMATICALLY WORK AT STRENGTHENING
LOW ABILITIES. THIS IS DONE THROUGH DR. MEEKER'S
PROCESS, BY MATCHING ONE LOW ABILITY WITH TWO
HIGH ABILITIES IN A LEARNING TASK (AN IMPORTANT
STRATEGY TO NOTE). A LEARNER IS ENCOURAGED BY
THE SUCCESS S/HE HAS IN THE TWO AREAS OF STRENGTH
WHILE S/HE CONTINUES WORKING TO DEVELOP AND BUILD
THE ONE AREA OF WEAKNESS.

THE ACTIVITIES IN THIS BOOK, <u>BUILDING BRAIN
POWER</u>, GIVE HEAVY EMPHASIS TO SKILLS AND ABILITIES
LEFT UNDEVELOPED IN TRADITIONAL EDUCATION. THESE
INCLUDE:

- DIVERGENT PRODUCTIVE THINKING OR CREATIVITY
- FORECASTING SKILLS
- APPLIED EVALUATION SKILLS
- DECISION MAKING
- 3-D OR SPATIAL THINKING
- APPLIED IMAGINATION
- CREATIVE PROBLEM SOLVING
- INTUITION
- MEMORY

166

MANY EDUCATORS THINK THEY TEACH IMAGINATION WHEN THEY SAY, "TODAY YOU MAY DRAW ANYTHING YOU WANT!" HOWEVER, THERE ARE TWO FALLACIES IN THIS. ONE, THE OPTION IS TOO BROAD. STUDENTS ARE UNABLE TO MAKE THE SHIFT FROM THE RIGID STRUCTURE DURING MOST OF THE DAY TO SUCH A WIDE OPEN GROUP OF CHOICES. MUCH LIKE ONE'S FIRST TRIP THROUGH A CAFETERIA LINE, THE LARGE NUMBER OF CHOICES CAN BE PARA-LYZING.

THE SECOND FALLACY LIES IN NOT MAKING A MEANINGFUL LINK FROM THE WIDE OPEN ASSIGN-MENT TO OTHER PARTS OF THE CURRICULUM. IMPLIED IN THIS IS A SUBTLE DISCOUNT. IN ORDER TO HAVE MEANING INITIALLY AND IN ORDER TO HAVE TRANSFER VALUE (A MEANINGFUL SKILL WHICH CAN LATER BE TRANSFERRED INTO USEFUL SERVICE ON DEMAND) THE STUDENT NEEDS TO UNDERSTAND HOW THIS PART (IMAGINATION) FITS WITH THE WHOLE OF LEARNING. THE STUDENT NEEDS TO LEARN HOW IMAGINATION, INTUITION, FANTASY ARE FORERUNNERS OF ALL PRACTICAL KNOWLEDGE AND HOW TO TAKE THEIR NEW IDEAS THROUGH THIS PROCESS OF REFINEMENT AND FINE TUNING. THE PROCESS GIVEN THROUGH THE BRAIN BUILDER SERIES IS DESIGNED TO LEAD BOTH THE TEACHER AND THE STUDENT, PARENT AND/OR ADULT AS LEARNER...THROUGH THE PROCESS WHILE SIMULTANEOUSLY LINKING IT TO RELEVANT AND VITAL SKILLS OF SUCCESSFUL LIVING.

THIS SECTION HAS BEEN ADAPTED FROM MATERIAL WRITTEN BY BETTY WATKINS FOR THE GIFTED STUDENTS INSTITUTE FOR RESEARCH AND DEVELOPMENT, 611 RYAN PLAZA DRIVE, SUITE 119, ARLINGTON, TEXAS 76011.

Designing a Brain Power Center

RESEARCH ON THE BRAIN AND ITS TWO HEMISPHERES OF OPPOSITE AND DIVERSE LEARNING POTENTIAL ENCOURAGES A STUDY OF CURRENT LEARNING STRATEGIES. MOST CLASSROOMS ARE LIMITED TO TWO-DIMENSIONAL MATERIALS SUCH AS PAPER, PENCILS, BOOKS, BLACKBOARDS. A PRIMARY BUT VITAL STEP TOWARD BROADENING CLASSROOM LEARNING TO STIMULATE AND DEVELOP MORE OF THE BI-LATERAL RESOURCES OF THE BRAIN WOULD BE TO INCREASE THE KINDS OF PROBLEM-SOLVING AND BASIC LEARNING MATERIALS THAT ARE AVAILABLE. BY PROVIDING A WIDE ASSORTMENT OF THREE-DIMENSIONAL MATERIALS, A RANGE OF TEXTURE, COLOR, SHAPE, SIZE, ETC., THE RIGHT SIDE OF THE BRAIN BECOMES MORE LIKELY TO BE USED AND SYSTEMATICALLY DEVELOPED ALONG WITH THE LEFT SIDE OF THE BRAIN. REMEMBER, THE ULTIMATE GOAL IS FOR

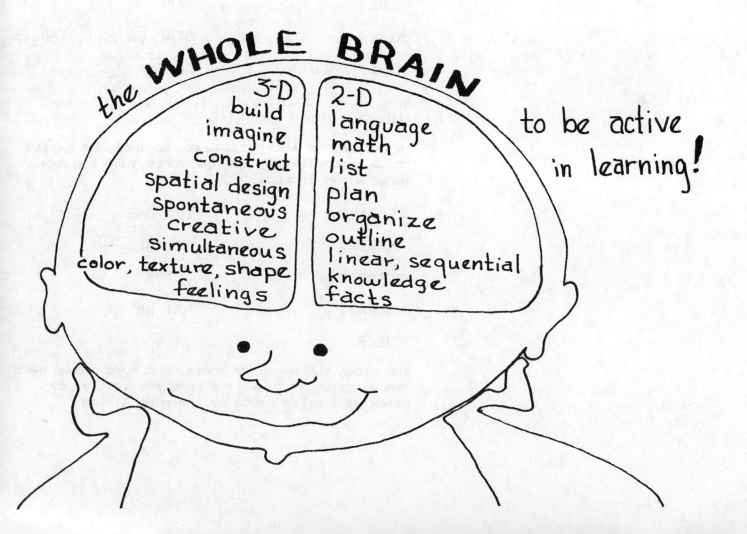

the WHOLE BRAIN

3-D
build
imagine
construct
spatial design
spontaneous
creative
simultaneous
color, texture, shape
feelings

2-D
language
math
list
plan
organize
outline
linear, sequential
knowledge
facts

to be active in learning!

LET'S BEGIN BY THINKING IN TERMS OF MAKING
SOME SPACE IN THE CLASSROOM, PERHAPS A CORNER, TO
SET UP RESOURCE MATERIALS THAT CAN BE USED AT ANY
TIME BY STUDENT OR TEACHER TO SOLVE OR WORK ON A
PROBLEM.   THE FREER EACH PERSON FEELS TO WALK OVER
AND USE MATERIALS TO EXPLAIN AN IDEA OR JUST TO
EXPAND ON PERSONAL DAYDREAMING AND WOOL GATHERING
THE MORE BENEFICIAL WILL BE THE RESOURCE OR BRAIN
POWER CENTER.

HERE IS A LIST OF MATERIALS YOU MIGHT WANT TO
COLLECT TO INCLUDE IN YOUR BRAIN POWER CENTER:

1. BONDING AGENTS

IN THE FIRST AREA, ORGANIZE ALL THE VARIOUS
MATERIALS YOU CAN FIND TO BOND OR ATTACH
ONE THING TO ANOTHER.   THESE WOULD BE
ITEMS SUCH AS:

STRING	PINS
PAPER CLIPS	PASTE
GLUE	TAPE
WIRE	STAPLER AND STAPLES
HOLE PUNCH	BRADS

2. TOOLS

IN THE SECOND AREA, ORGANIZE (SO THEY ARE EASILY
FOUND AND PUT AWAY) ALL THE TOOLS THAT YOU CAN.
THESE MIGHT INCLUDE:

PENCILS	CRAYONS
MARKERS	BRUSHES
SCISSORS	CLIPS
COMPASS	MAT KNIFE
RULER	

THE WIDER THE RANGE OF TOOLS, THE MORE IDEAS THAT
CAN BE STIMULATED AND THE MORE POSSIBILITY OF
REACHING A WIDER RANGE OF LEARNING STYLES.

3. MATERIALS

IN THE THIRD AREA ORGANIZE AS MANY TWO-DIMENSIONAL AND THREE-DIMENSIONAL MATERIALS FROM WHICH TO CREATE, BUILD, DESIGN AND PROBLEM-SOLVE AS YOU CAN. THESE MIGHT INCLUDE:

NEWSPRINT	EGG CARTONS
MANILLA PAPER	BOXES, ALL SIZES (CAN BE BROKEN DOWN AND STORED FLAT)
COLORED PAPER	
CARDBOARD	FABRIC SCRAPS
WRAPPING PAPER	YARN, STRING
TISSUE PAPER	LACE, RIBBON
TOILET PAPER ROLLS	STYROFOAM
SCRAP WOOD	PLASTIC COVERS, BOTTLES, LIDS
NEWSPAPERS	SPOOLS
MAGAZINES	

NOTE: #1. THIS TYPE OF PLANNING AND ORGANIZATION IS TYPICALLY DONE BY THE TEACHER. YOU CAN MORE THAN DOUBLE THE IMPACT AND VALUE OF THIS APPROACH TO LEARNING BY INVOLVING THE STUDENTS IN THE PLANNING AND ORGANIZATION OF THIS BRAIN POWER CENTER. THE MORE INITIATIVE STUDENTS OF ANY AGE TAKE IN COLLECTING AND ORGANIZING THESE MATERIALS, WORK SPACES AND ORGANIZATIONAL SYSTEMS, THE MORE LEARNING IS TAKING PLACE. HELPING TO COLLECT THESE MATERIALS WILL RAISE AWARENESS OF WHAT IS AROUND TO BE COLLECTED AND WHAT IS AVAILABLE TO BE USED. DAILY, WE THROW AWAY ALL SORTS OF INTERESTING OBJECTS AND RESOURCES THAT COULD FEED OUR IMAGINATION AND PROBLEM-SOLVING ABILITY. ALSO,

STUDENTS CAN EXERCISE IMPORTANT LEARNING SKILLS
SUCH AS TO:

ANALYZE

ORGANIZE

CATEGORIZE

PLAN

MANAGE

EVALUATE

RE-ARRANGE

STUDENTS GET A DIFFERENT MESSAGE ABOUT THE
CLASSROOM WHEN THEY TAKE AN ACTIVE ROLL IN
THE MANAGEMENT AND DESIGN OF IT.

THIS GIVES STUDENTS PERMISSION TO ORIGINATE AS
WELL AS TO FOLLOW THE LEAD. IT ENCOURAGES AND
FOSTERS INITIATIVE . IT DEVELOPS LEADERSHIP
AND A MORE ACTIVE, SELF-DIRECTED FORM OF
LEARNING.

NOTE: #2, USUALLY ONLY AN ART ROOM, KINDER-
GARTEN OR PRIMARY CLASSROOM MIGHT HAVE SUCH A RANGE
OF "ART" MATERIALS. BY MAKING THESE AVAILABLE
GENERALLY TO ALL AGES LEARNING AND CREATIVITY
CAN BE INCREASED. IN UPPER LEVELS OF MATH,
SCIENCE, LANGUAGE, BIOLOGY...ALL OF THE FIELDS OF
LEARNING CAN BE EXPANDED TO INCLUDE A WHOLE-
BRAIN INVOLVEMENT BY INCLUDING A RESOURCE
CENTER APPROACH. THIS IS A WAY OF STIMULATING

AND FACILITATING THE

WOOLGATHERING THAT LEADS TO **LINKING**

THAT IS ESSENTIAL FOR

IN FACT, ONE OF THE MORE EFFECTIVE WAYS TO JAR NEW THINKING IS TO HAVE UNEXPECTED THINGS IN UNEXPECTED PLACES. WHEN HELPING TOP EXECUTIVES IN BUSINESS TO LEARN CREATIVE PROBLEM-SOLVING, I OFTEN BRING IN TOYS SUCH AS GIANT TINKER TOYS, MARKERS AND LARGE PAPER. THE SAME APPROACH WAS HIGHLY PRODUCTIVE IN TEACHING POST DOCTORAL CANDIDATES IN SCIENCE AND TECHNOLOGY TO RE-AWAKEN THEIR CREATIVITY. IT SEEMS THAT THESE MATERIALS APPEAL TO THE SLEEPING CHILD WITHIN EACH OF US AND INVITES THIS

OPENLY PLAYFUL,

HIGHLY CURIOUS,

HIGHLY CREATIVE,

NATURAL ENGINEER,

INVENTIVE, INGENIUS PROBLEM-SOLVER

TO JOIN WITH THE SOPHISTICATED, DISCIPLINED HIGHLY DEVELOPED, WELL-TRAINED ADULT MIND WHICH CAN GREATLY INCREASE YOUR TOTAL POTENTIAL.

Glossary

ASSYMETRICAL - UNEQUAL ARRANGEMENT OF PARTS ON OPPOSITE SIDES OF A PLANE OR LINE.

BIONICS - APPLYING OBSERVATIONS OF NATURE TO MAN-MADE THINGS.

BRAINSTORMING - A PROCESS OF FREE, UNREFINED THINKING USED BY A GROUP OF PEOPLE TO GENERATE MANY CREATIVE IDEAS WITHOUT INTERFERENCE OR JUDGMENT.

CARTOGRAPHY - THE ART OF MAPPING.

CONCEPTUAL REPATTERNING - CREATIVE PROBLEM-SOLVING.

CRITERIA - "YARDSTICK" FOR MAKING DECISIONS OR CHOICES.

CRYPTOGRAPH - SOMETHING WRITTEN IN CODE OR CIPHER.

E.S.P. - EXTRA SENSORY PERCEPTION.

HITCHHIKING - A PROCESS OF GENERATING ONE IDEA BY THE SUBMISSION OF ANOTHER.

IMAGERY - THINKING THROUGH PICTURES OR IMAGES. SEEING AN IDEA AS A PICTURE.

IMAGINATION BUILDERS - ANY EXPERIENCE WHICH STIMULATES THE DEVELOPMENT OF THE IMAGINATION.

IMAGINATION STRETCHERS - EXTENDING AN IDEA TO NEW DIMENSIONS.

INTUITION - THE PROCESS OF KNOWING WITHOUT KNOWING HOW YOU KNOW.

LATERAL THINKING - NON-DIRECTIONAL THINKING LETTING IMAGINATION RATHER THAN LOGIC DIRECT THOUGHTS.

PIGGYBACKING - ANOTHER TERM FOR HITCHHIKING. ONE IDEA SUGGESTS ANOTHER.

PO - A WORD TO BLOCK INTERFERENCE WITH LATERAL THINKING.

SYMMETRICAL - EQUAL ARRANGEMENT OF PARTS ON OPPOSITE SIDES OF A PLANE OR LINE.

VERTICAL THINKING - LOGICAL, GOAL-ORIENTED THINKING.

WOOLGATHERING - LETTING THE MIND WANDER, BEING CURIOUS, COLLECTING IDEAS FOR NO IMMEDIATE REASON BUT FOR LATER USE.

Further Resources

THE ACT OF CREATION. KOESTLER, ARTHUR, DELL, NEW YORK, (PAPERBACK), 1964. THE MACMILLAN CO., NEW YORK, 1967.

A 5-DAY COURSE IN THINKING. DE BONO, EDWARD.

AHA! INSIGHT. GARDNER, MARTIN, SCIENTIFIC AMERICAN, INC./ W.H. FREEMAN AND COMPANY, NEW YORK CITY/SAN FRANCISCO.

AMERICAN DENIM: A NEW FOLK ART. TEXT BY PETER BEAGLE, HARRY N. ABRAMS, NEW YORK, 1975.

APPLIED IMAGINATION. OSBORN, ALEX, SCRIBNERS, NEW YORK.

CALDER'S CIRCUS. EDITED BY JEAN LIPMAN WITH NANCY FOOTE, E.P. DUTTON AND COMPANY, INC., NEW YORK.

CONCEPTUAL BLOCKBUSTING: A GUIDE TO BETTER IDEAS. SECOND EDITION, ADAMS, JAMES L., W.W. NORTON AND COMPANY, NEW YORK.

CREATIVITY: ITS EDUCATIONAL IMPLICATIONS. GOWAN, JOHN C., DEMOS, GEORGE D., AND TORRANCE, E. PAUL (EDITORS), JOHN WILEY AND SONS, NEW YORK, (PAPERBACK), 1967.

CREATIVITY AND ITS EDUCATIONAL IMPLICATIONS FOR THE GIFTED. "THE GIFTED CHILD QUARTERLY", TORRANCE, E. PAUL, 1968.

CREATIVITY AND LEARNING. KAGAN, JEROME (EDITOR), (PAPER-BACK), 1967. BEACON PRESS, BOSTON, MASSACHUSETTS.

CREATIVITY--THE MAGIC SYNTHESIS. ARIETI, SILVANO, BASIC BOOKS, INC., NEW YORK, 1976.

THE COURAGE TO CREATE. MAY, ROLLO, W.W. NORTON, COMPANY, NEW YORK, 1975. BANTAM, NEW YORK, (PAPERBACK), 1977.

DESIGN YOURSELF! HANKS, KURT, BELLISTON, LARRY, EDWARDS, DAVE, WILLIAMS KAUFMAN, INC., LOS ALTOS, CALIFORNIA.

DEVELOPING ARTISTIC & PERCEPTUAL AWARENESS. ART PRACTICE IN THE ELEMENTARY CLASSROOM, THIRD EDITION, LINDERMAN, EARL W., HERBERHOLZ, DONALD W., WILLIAM C. BROWN COMPANY, 1974.

178

FABLES OF AESOP. WITH 50 DRAWINGS BY ALEXANDER CALDWELL.
    DOVER PUBLICATIONS, INC., NEW YORK.

GROWING UP GIFTED. DEVELOPING THE POTENTIAL OF CHILDREN
    AT HOME AND AT SCHOOL. CLARK, BARBARA, CALIFORNIA STATE
    UNIVERSITY, CHARLES E. MERRILL PUBLISHING COMPANY.

HANDMADE HOUSES. A GUIDE TO THE WOODBUTCHER'S ART.
    BOERICKE, ART AND SHAPIRO, BARRY, A AND W VISUAL LIBRARY,
    1973.

IMAGINEERING. HOW TO PROFIT FROM YOUR CREATIVE POWERS.
    LEBOUF, MICHAEL, MCGRAW-HILL BOOK COMPANY, NEW YORK.

LATERAL THINKING. CREATIVITY STEP BY STEP. DE BONO, EDWARD,
    HARPER COLOPHON BOOKS/CN 325.

THE MANAGEMENT OF INTELLIGENCE--SCIENTIFIC PROBLEM SOLVING
    AND CREATIVITY. GREGORY, CARL E., MCGRAW-HILL BOOK COMPANY,
    NEW YORK, 1967.

MASQUERADE. WILLIAMS, KIT, SCHOKEN BOOKS, NEW YORK.

THE NATURE OF HUMAN INTELLIGENCE. GUILFORD, J.P., MCGRAW-
    HILL BOOK COMPANY, NEW YORK, 1967.

NEW THINK. THE USE OF LATERAL THINKING IN THE GENERATION
    OF NEW IDEAS. DE BONO, EDWARD, BASIC BOOKS, INC., NEW YORK.

PO: A DEVICE FOR SUCCESSFUL THINKING. DE BONO, EDWARD,
    SIMON AND SCHUSTER, NEW YORK, 1972.

THE ROAD TO ZANADU--A STUDY IN THE WAYS OF THE IMAGINATION.
    LOWES, JOHN LIVINGSTON, VINTAGE BOOKS, NEW YORK, (PAPERBACK),
    1959.

THE SEARCH FOR SOLUTIONS. JUELSON, HORACE FREELAND, HOLT,
    RINEHART & WINSTON COMPANY, NEW YORK.

THE SEWING MACHINE AS A CREATIVE TOOL. BAKKE, KAREN, PRENTICE-
    HALL, 1976.

THE STRENGTH TO DREAM--LITERATURE AND THE IMAGINATION.
WILSON, COLIN, HOUGHTON, MIFFLIN & COMPANY, BOSTON,
1962.

SUPER LEARNING. OSTRANDER, SHEILA AND SCHROEDER, LYNN,
WITH NANCY OSTRANDER, DELACOURTE PRESS/CONFUCIAN PRESS,
NEW YORK.

THE TECHNIQUES OF CREATIVE THINKING. HOW TO USE YOUR
IDEAS TO ACHIEVE SUCCESS. CRAWFORD, ROBERT P.,
HAWTHORN BOOKS, NEW YORK, (PAPERBACK), 1966.

THINK TANKS. DICKSON, PAUL, BALLANTINE BOOKS, NEW YORK,
(PAPERBACK), 1971.

THE THREE BOXES OF LIFE AND HOW TO GET OUT OF THEM. AN
INTRODUCTION TO LIFE/WORK PLANNING. BOLLES, RICHARD N.,
TEN SPEED PRESS.

THE UNIVERSAL TRAVELER. A SOFT-SYSTEM GUIDE TO: CREATIVITY,
PROBLEM-SOLVING AND THE PROCESS OF REACHING GOALS.
KOBERG, DON AND BAGALL, JIM, WILLIAM KAUFMAN, INC.

USE BOTH SIDES OF YOUR BRAIN. BUZAN, TONY, E.P. DUTTON
COMPANY, NEW YORK.

WIDENING HORIZONS IN CREATIVITY. TAYLOR, CALVIN W.,
JOHN WILEY & SONS, NEW YORK, 1964.

I HIGHLY RECOMMEND THAT PARENTS OF GIFTED STUDENTS CONTACT THE
GIFTED STUDENTS INSTITUTE, 611 RYAN PLAZA DRIVE, SUITE 1119, ARLINGTON,
TEXAS 76011, FOR INFORMATION ON PROGRAMS AVAILABLE NATIONALLY AND OTHER
SERVICES FOR THE GIFTED.

About the Author

DR. ANN MCGEE-COOPER HOLDS DEGREES FROM SEVERAL UNIVERSITIES INCLUDING THE UNIVERISTIY OF TEXAS AT AUSTIN IN DESIGN; SOUTHERN METHODIST UNIVERSITY IN THE RELATED ARTS, CREATIVITY IN TEACHING; COLUMBIA UNIVERSITY IN THE ARTS AND EDUCATION. SHE HAS DONE ADVANCED STUDY AT PURDUE UNIVERSITY, PENN STATE UNIVERSITY AND DREW SEMINARY.

WHILE TEACHING AT SOUTHERN METHODIST UNIVERSITY SHE FOUNDED THE EXPERIMENTAL ARTS PROGRAM, A MODEL TEACHER TRAINING PROGRAM RECOGNIZED NATIONALLY FOR SIGNIFICANT INNOVATIONS IN EDUCATION. HER DOCTORATE AT TEACHERS COLLEGE, COLUMBIA UNIVERSITY WAS FOCUSED ON A TEACHER SURVIVAL PROGRAM SHE FOUNDED WITH HER COLLEAGUES IN THE EXPERIMENTAL ARTS PROGRAM. THE FOCUS OF THIS RESEARCH WAS POSITIVE ALTERNATIVES TO TEACHER AND STUDENT BURN-OUT. MUCH OF BUILDING BRAIN POWER REFLECTS THIS RESEARCH.

HER RESEARCH AND CONSULTING IN THE FIELD OF CREATIVITY, THE PRACTICAL APPLICATIONS OF EXPANSIVE THINKING AND HUMAN BEHAVIOR, BEGAN IN 1953 AND EXPANDED DIRECTLY INTO SCIENCE, TECHNOLOGY AND BUSINESS. SHE HAS SERVED AS A CONSULTANT AND SPEAKER TO NATIONAL CONFERENCES IN THE FIELDS OF EDUCATION INCLUDING THE ARTS, READING, LEARNING DISABILITIES AND GIFTED EDUCATION. SHE ALSO CONSULTS WITH BUSINESS IN THE FIELDS OF FUTURISM, CREATIVITY, EXPANSIVE THINKING, MOTIVATION AND CONCEPTUAL REPATTERNING.

SHE WAS NAMED ONE OF THE OUTSTANDING YOUNG EDUCATORS IN AMERICA, 1973 AND AN OUTSTANDING PROFESSOR AT SMU, 1975. CURRENTLY SHE SERVES AS TEACHER, WRITER, SPEAKER, ARTIST, CONSULTANT AND SPECIALIST IN EXPANSIVE THINKING.